Group Exercises for Substance Use Disorders Counseling

Group Exercises for Substance Use Disorders Counseling

Second Edition

Geri Miller

*This book is dedicated to Ron Hood, my husband and friend, who once again
has been my steadfast partner through the writing of this book; to Gale, Abby, and
Jason Miller, and Tom, Laura, Natalie, and Kate Prow; Zoe, Anrai, and
Corina Schriver—my families whom I treasure; to my personal counselors and fellow
group members who years ago helped me learn how to live better in this world through their
loving confrontation of me in a community of support; and to the clients I have had the
honor of counseling in SUD groups.*

Contents

Preface

The first edition of this book evolved from a dinner conversation with an experienced SUD counselor years ago who said, "This is a book [a workbook on group counseling] that needs to be written for SUD counselors." I remembered these words of Jane Albers, whom I respect and care for both personally and professionally. At the time, it felt like the first edition of this book came full circle when she agreed to be a reviewer of the first edition. The second edition of this book came from an invitation of my Wiley editor, Darren Lalonde, to write an update of the book. Because I believe in the power of group work for the SUD population and enjoy my work with Darren, I agreed to write a second edition.

I have always drawn on my personal experiences, as a group member in group counseling, to remind me of the importance of a leader providing care, respect, and honesty to clients and creating an atmosphere in a group that is conducive to those factors. I was blessed to have those experiences as a client where group leaders and fellow group members helped me learn, in a supportive community, about my blind and hidden spots that were causing me problems in living.

Since I began working as a mental health professional in 1976, I have been involved in group work. As a counselor, I found it fascinating and powerful and have tried to incorporate it into every professional job I have had. In my Master's degree program, I studied group work beyond classroom assignments, and my doctoral internship was in a counseling center that emphasized group counseling. Much of my counseling in the SUD field has been in group counseling. I have been privileged both personally and professionally to witness the healing power of groups in all of the settings in which I have worked, and specifically, I have seen miracles of change in the lives of SUD clients and their loved ones as a result of group counseling.

The first edition of this book of exercises evolved from trainings (over a number of years) that I conducted beginning in 1999 with experienced SUD counselors where each training participant described one of their favorite group counseling exercises. I chose specific exercises from this wealth of counselor experiences and described them in a concise, almost recipe-like format for the reader. The goal of the first edition of this book became to have tried-and-true exercises readily available for busy SUD clinicians. The second edition has built on this cornerstone of counselor experiences as numerous consultants (14 individual counselors and 1 group of counselors), who used the first edition in their SUD counseling work, provided me with feedback from March 2023 through December 2024. They critiqued the first edition and made suggestions on how to update the second edition.

The second edition of this book is divided into the same four sections as the first edition (with numerous changes throughout), and the following is a brief summary of each section:

- **Section 1, Introduction**, provides an overview of the rationale of the workbook.
- **Section 2, Philosophy and Practice of Group Work**, is divided into two areas: an excerpt from my book, *Learning the Language of Addiction Counseling* (5th edition) (2021), that provides my philosophy of group work with SUD clients and their loved ones; and four "Words to the Wise" sections that focus on core, critical areas of group counseling that are needed to encourage healing from SUD.
- **Section 3, Group Exercises**, has a personal reflections section added and provides specific exercises (separated into 10 categories) that can be used in group counseling: Icebreakers; SUD Recovery; Family/Relationships/Culture; Feelings Exploration; Group Community Building; Self-Esteem; Recovery Skills: Communication/Mindfulness/Problem Solving; Values; Openers; and Closers. These exercises have been reorganized into in-person or online version categories.

◆ **Section 4, Resources**, has been divided into two sections: Current Favorites (2nd edition) and Classic Favorites (1st edition). The Current Favorites section has an expansion of readings that includes general group readings as well as readings on music, transgender, and yoga; workbooks/exercises; icebreaker exercises divided into those with a group therapy focus and those with an individual therapy focus; and an expanded website section (e.g., general; music therapy; transgender).

Geri Miller, Ph.D.
Boone, North Carolina
25 April 2025

Acknowledgments

I have had numerous excellent teachers in the counseling field who have been my mentors, supervisors, colleagues, and students. I am deeply grateful for the time and energy each one of you invested in teaching me about group counseling in the area of SUD. Through watching your practice of honesty, openness, and willingness, as you examined your strengths and weaknesses both personally and professionally, I learned and continue to learn how to be a better person in this world and how to be a part of the one human community to which we all belong.

I especially thank the SUD clients and their loved ones who I witnessed being brave in group counseling, daring to be different, and as a result, healing from and learning to live with the wounds of the storylines of their lives. Your courageous stories have taught me how to live and encouraged me to continue to believe in the amazing power of the human spirit and its capacity for change, especially in the context of a community of support. Your stories are the miracles I have witnessed that sustain me personally and professionally and are a wellspring of hope that I am able to pass on to others in my personal life and professional work.

I also want to thank my personal group counselors and fellow group members I crossed paths with years ago who helped me look at my blind and hidden spots as a human being and thereby invited me into a new way of living. Thank you for being a part of saving my life. We had quite an adventure together, and I am grateful to each of you for being my buddies on that journey.

In the first edition of this book that laid the foundation for this second edition, I thanked the North Carolina Foundation for Alcohol and Drug Studies (NCFADS) Board and its executive director, Dr. Jim Edmundson, who invited me to be a trainer of group counseling skills, at their winter and summer schools, year after year. These opportunities allowed me to practice what I love (group counseling) with those I respect (SUD counselors), counselors who are working hard to be a part of saving the lives of SUD clients and their loved ones who are suffering with the disease of SUD. In the first edition, I gave a special thank you to Jane Albers, who encouraged me over dinner to write this book years before it was published and then served as a reviewer of the first edition. In this second edition, I thank the previous executive director of NCFADS, Sarah Cothren, who encouraged SUD counselors to learn about SUD group work by inviting me to conduct a mini-track training at the 2024 NCFADS summer school followed up by a 2025 NCFADS winter school main track training. I also want to thank Beth Harmer, the president of the NCFADS Board, who took on the additional role of executive director during the 2025 NCFADS winter school and who, along with the NCFADS Board, assisted me immensely during the school. The picture of me hula hooping in Section 3 was taken during one of the training school breaks by Michael Roberts, director of outreach for the Addiction Professionals of North Carolina (APNC)-thank you Michael for your thoughtfulness in capturing a fun training moment. Finally, I want to thank the experienced counselor participants in my April 2025 Northwest Area Health Education Center (NWAHEC) group counseling workshop that was coordinated by Ellen Kesler, Continuing Education Coordinator (Behavioral Health). These counselors generously contributed "twists" to a couple of exercises in Section 3.

I also want to thank the consultants who worked with me to make this book more sensitive to diversity within SUD clients, different settings of groups (e.g., inpatient, outpatient), different types of groups (e.g., harm reduction, abstinence-based), and different group formats (in-person, online, hybrid). These individuals freely and enthusiastically gave me their feedback in person, Zoom, or email because they believed in the importance of group work in the SUD field. Their views are expressed in each section of this book, especially in Section 3 where they drew on their expert clinical experience. I chose my consultants carefully—counselors whose group work I respect because they always put the welfare of the client first. These consultants were Eli Ahamed, Christopher Byrd, Emily Capps, Tuesday Ferral, Dale Hudler, Jeff Hunsucker, Kathryn Hunsucker, Andrea Marsh, Katelyn Monday, Emily Proctor, Kayla Reber, Sara Shook-Rosen, Wiley Smith, and Stephanie Perez Toro. To them I say: "We wrote a book together to help people heal."

Additionally, I want to thank the people at John Wiley & Sons, Inc., who helped me write this book in so many ways: Darren Lalonde, my editor, who has helped me be the best writer I could be on this book and on previous books—Darren has extensive experience and knowledge as an editor that is balanced with his deep support and commitment to his authors—with me he waited patiently for over 2 years for this book to be completed and met with me at my request to discuss plans and extensions on the book publishing deadline; Pascal Raj Francois, my managing editor, who met with Darren and me initially and then individually met with me regularly to provide me with support and encouragement as the publication deadline approached—he answered my questions promptly and found ways to make my dream of this book to come true (e.g., inclusion of the graphic cartoon in the text); and Christina Weyrauch, Senior Editorial Assistant, who responded quickly and kindly to requests I made that assisted me in writing this book and like Darren and Pascal, believed in me and the importance of this work. During the final months of writing this book, Hurricane Helene struck the mountains of North Carolina where I live. Darren and Pascal kept telling me to not worry about the book deadline but encouraged me to take care of myself, my loved ones, and the community in which I live. Christina joined them in their support of me through this difficult time. The deep care and support from all three of them sustained me in writing this book when my time and energy was so depleted by the horrific disaster. I will always be in their debt for their belief in me and this work as well as their deep compassion and concern for me, my loved ones, and my mountain community. Additionally, I thank the entire Wiley Production Team, especially L. Mary Angelin Rose, Content Refinement Specialist, who patiently and efficiently guided this book through its production phase—her dedication to the quality of this book encouraged me to continue working on the book.

There are numerous other employees behind the scenes at Wiley who helped me, and I thank each of you. One of these individuals is Patty Maher in marketing who has assisted me on previous books with her intelligence, honesty, and hard work. Thank you for making sure this book reaches those individuals who find it helpful in their SUD work.

A special thank you to Olive Barry, my cartoon graphic designer who also worked as my research assistant—Olive is a bright, kind, and hardworking person with a delightful sense of humor, and Emily Proctor, my research assistant throughout the book and specifically on Section 4—Emily is also bright, kind, and hardworking with a delightful sense of humor. Both of these individuals brought joy, laughter, and support to me as we worked together on this book. A special thank you to Reese Wells, for his kindness, patience, and brilliance in creating a podcast for this book, and Ron Hood who served as a cameraperson for the video that accompanies this book.

I also need to thank my computer teacher/collaborator, George Dennis, who is bright, kind, funny, patient, flexible, honest, and reliable. These traits in combination with his constant support and belief in me and my work made the first and second editions of this book possible.

I also thank my friends who I consider family: Dawn and Gerald Houck; Bruce Kaplan and JoJo Muldoon (and their dog Amina who joined their family during the writing of this book); Laurie Percival Oates; and Marilou, Richard, Alan, and Lorie Steinmetz; each of whom showed me kindness, compassion, and support in the safe havens they provided for me in the writing of this book. I also thank my Saturday morning coffee drinking buddies, who continue to believe in me personally and professionally and help me "live life on life's terms" and insist on enjoying life with them through humor and laughter.

And an extra special thank you to Ron Hood, my husband and best friend, who read every word of every draft of this book and gave up weekend and evening time with me so I could work on the book. In so many ways, I truly could not have written this book without you. My thank you remains the same as it has been in other books I have written: "Thank you, Ron, for being with me on this life path. I love you." And thank you to Ginger, our 4-year-old American Fox Hound dog that joined us (and our 5-year-old all black cat named Hope) this past year from the local animal shelter teaching us patience and making us laugh.

About the Companion Website

This book is accompanied by both instructor and student companion website.

www.wiley.com/go/miller/sud2e 

This website includes:

Instructor website:

- Considerations for Professors
- PPTs
- Test Bank

Student website:

- Cartoon Graphics
- Link to Videos
- Link to Podcast

1

Introduction

PERSONAL REFLECTIONS

The first and second editions of this book have a lot of meaning for me personally as well as professionally. I believe that group therapy, as practiced by experienced, trained counselors, saved my life—which is why I am writing a book about it. In group therapy, I learned, in the moment when I was engaging in specific behaviors, exactly which behaviors were inhibiting my ability to connect effectively with others and to set up a community of support with others. That is a nice way of saying that counselors and fellow clients confronted me on destructive behavior when I was doing it, and I could hear, see, and feel the impact of that behavior on others through their confrontation of me. I hated group therapy because I lived in fear of it. I was terrified of learning about my blind spots and hidden spots and having them pointed out in front of others. However, I also felt cared about in group therapy. Counselors and other clients cared enough about me to tell me hard things—hard things for them to say, hard things for me to hear. People took risks to tell me things that I did not want to hear and cared enough about me to extend their own vulnerability as

Group Exercises for Substance Use Disorders Counseling, Second Edition. Geri Miller.
© 2025 John Wiley & Sons, Inc. Published 2025 by John Wiley & Sons, Inc.
Companion website: www.wiley.com/go/miller/sud2e

expressed in their honesty. They also nurtured me and supported me after the confrontation and reminded me that progress, not perfection, is important in living.

I learned a lot about myself in group therapy that has helped me immeasurably to live and work with others in the world. I came out of the experience knowing my flaws as well as my strengths. I believe it is easier for me to live in the world and, hopefully, easier for others to live with me after the experience of group therapy. That is why I believe in the importance of this book. My hope is that counselors can find in these tried-and-true group exercises ways to help their clients understand themselves better, thereby offering them more choices about how they can live their lives and break out of dysfunctional interaction patterns with others. My simple hope is that the techniques may be used by counselors to help their clients live better.

Prior to a discussion of the main points of this chapter, I would like to make comments about *two populations and two approaches* that I have chosen a few to highlight here because of my experience in working in the substance use disorders (SUD) field. With regard to populations, specific SUD-related issues may arise in terms of population (e.g., transgender; trauma survivors) and approaches (e.g., yoga; music).

Regarding the *transgender population*, specific comments on working with this population are made in Sections 2, 3, and 4 of this book. In Section 4, transgender resources are listed. An example from the transgender resource section and how counselors may use this resource follows. The Substance Abuse and Mental Health Services Administration (SAMHSA, 2024) published "Behavioral Health of Adolescents across Sexual Identities" that summarized the results from the 2023 National Survey on Drug Use and Health. This publication highlights the struggles of LGB+ adolescents. While there is public support for LGB+ individuals, there continues to be mental health and substance use disparities for LGB+ youth. This population has more behavioral health issues when compared to their heterosexual (straight) peers that include depression, suicidality, and substance use. They also experience bullying and discrimination that can contribute to their substance use and mental health status. Social support and strategies for coping can enhance their resilience.

Counselors can use the information in this resource to assist their LGB+ adolescents in understanding the common struggles they may experience (e.g., mental health, substance use). They can also provide them with social support and coping strategies that can assist them in becoming and staying sober as well as improving their mental health.

Because many SUD clients are *trauma survivors*, I want to make a few comments about working in this area. First, trauma survivors may be sensitive to criticism, concerned about upsetting others, fearful that those individuals they are close to may leave them, and struggle with not feeling as though they are enough. Second, when their trauma is triggered, they may want to use; want to hurt themselves or others; have strong overwhelming emotional reactions of fear/anger/guilt/shame; and be unable to make themselves feel safe. The "solution" may be to help them feel safe, calm themselves down through their senses, and talk out their trauma reaction with someone they trust (e.g., counselor, self-help group sponsor) who understands their trauma and can reassure them it will not last forever. Spirituality, in terms of one's existence, may help empower sexual abuse trauma survivors move on from the trauma (Skalski-Bednarz & Toussaint, 2024). For example, spiritual practices such as contemplative/meditative ones can result in a healing that is deeper than the wounds of their trauma (Adams, 2025). Overall, however, counselors need to also be aware that their clients may have experienced religious/spiritual trauma that impacts their self-identity, core beliefs/values, and sense of safety in the world along with their sense of the sacred (Walsh & Koch, 2023). Exercises used to work with them need to be chosen thoughtfully and carefully always respecting their limits and yet asking them to "stretch" themselves. Motivational interviewing theory and techniques may be especially helpful in working with them.

There are two approaches highlighted here, *yoga and 12-step recovery* and *music therapy*. These two approaches can serve as an example of approaches the clinician may use in conjunction with the exercises provided in this book.

Yoga and 12-Step Recovery

In the research domain, for twenty years, there has been an increase in yoga for health research while in the general public domain there has been an increased interest in and involvement with yoga (Wasson et al., 2024). Such research and public interests require the inclusion of yoga in a discussion of SUD recovery.

The following paragraphs are a summary of Greene's (2021) article pertaining to the use of yoga as an increasingly used approach in SUD treatment and recovery. Yoga is a holistic practice that involves the integration of the body, mind, and spirit (e.g., breath, life force).

In terms of 12-step recovery, SUD is described as a biopsychosocial-spiritual disorder in mutual aid recovery communities such as Alcoholics Anonymous (AA) and

Narcotics Anonymous (NA). A reality for SUD clients in early recovery is that they need to let go of their substance-using social networks that they had when actively using substances; they need to establish a new recovery social network through groups such as AA and NA. A part of a new recovery social network, augmenting the 12-step recovery groups, could include the yoga community of practice.

Yoga is showing promising research results in the treatment of SUD. Systematic research reviews have been done to examine yoga's impact on SUD recovery and have shown promising results in terms of a decrease in both cravings (the most powerful relapse risk factor) and negative mood states that are a part of the disease. This main impact on cognition (e.g., cravings, negative mood states) may be related to the mindfulness encouraged in the practice of yoga.

Music Therapy and SUD Treatment

Music is enjoyable and has been shown in the research that it is good for one's mind, heart, and soul (Mehegan & Rainville, 2020). Specifically, it:

- provides fun and pleasure;
- increases a sense of well-being;
- reduces stress;
- modulates the cardiovascular system;
- improves balance;
- boosts the immune system; and
- enhances interpersonal connections (Global Council on Brain Health, 2020).

The Global Council on Brain Health (2020) suggests tapping the healing power of music whether through dancing, singing, or movement-these activities will reduce stress, provide physical activity, and create opportunities to socialize. The link for their publication is included at the end of this chapter and in Section 4 of this book.

In 2021, the American Music Therapy Association, Inc. (AMTA) published an article on music therapy and SUD treatment. The link for this article is included in Section 4 of this book. AMTA states that music can be a part of an integrated approach to SUD treatment and used in the context of the therapeutic relationship. Also, music has been shown to activate dopaminergic pathways in a similar manner to alcohol/drugs.

The benefits that SUD clients may experience from music include the following:

- promoting connection within themselves and motivating them to stay sober;
- reducing cravings and improving mood; and
- encouraging relaxation and decreasing anxiety.

However, contraindications of the use of music include triggering trauma and/or alcohol/drug use as well as increasing cravings for alcohol/drugs.

In summary, counselors need to remember to practice in their area of competence. *First*, that means that unless the counselor is also a music therapist, music needs to be integrated into the therapeutic relationship the counselor has with each member of the group in the group setting as well as the entire group. Because one of the ways in which clients remember what they learn in counseling is through music, specific music-related exercises are listed in Section 3. *Second*, if contraindications to the music occur for anyone in the group, it is important to stop the music and process what happened in the group. Such actions teach clients that they need to take the same action if they experience contraindications to music outside the group setting. *Finally*, counselors need to work closely/consult with a music therapist about using music in their group counseling.

MAIN SECTION POINTS

1. SUD is a significant problem.
2. Treatment of SUD requires a biopsychosocial perspective and a balance of grassroots-based assistance and research findings.
3. This book is a complementary book to *Learning the Language of Addiction Counseling* (5th ed.) (2021), containing exercises used by experienced SUD counselors.
4. Group therapy is commonly used in SUD treatment because it offers interpersonal learning, a community of support, cost-effectiveness, and a history of effectiveness with SUD clients and their loved ones.
5. Counselors are encouraged to adapt these exercises to their own practice.

OVERVIEW

The SUD problem in the United States has reached alarming significance. In 2020, a total of 92,000 Americans died from drug overdose deaths (30% more than in 2019 and 75% more than in the last 5 years) making it the highest annual total on record according to the Center for Disease Control (CDC) (Gramlich, 2022). The Substance Abuse and Mental Health Services Administration (SAMHSA) found in their 2020 survey results that 58.7% of individuals 12 years or older reported that in the last month, they had used tobacco, alcohol, or an illicit drug (SAMHSA, 2021b) and in their 2023 survey (SAMHSA, 2025) found that for individuals 12 or older, 45.5 million people had an SUD in the past year; 28.9 million had an alcohol disorder (AUD); 27.2 million had a drug use disorder (DUD); and 7.5 million had both an AUD and a DUD. However, they also found in the 2023 survey (SAMHSA, 2025), that most individuals who could benefit from treatment do not receive it due to barriers such as financial (e.g., insurance); transportation; provider limitations (e.g., shortage of providers) and administrative requirements. This widespread problem results in many clients having an active or historical problem with SUD themselves or having family members who have struggled with SUD. If clients have not had to address SUD in themselves or their family members, they often are aware of someone in their daily lives (e.g., boss, friend, neighbor) whose SUD problem impacts their life. Because many clients are impacted by SUD, all counselors need to have the skills to work effectively with these issues. Counselors who work primarily in mental health settings need to be prepared to work with these issues that these clients bring to counseling, as well as SUD counselors who work directly with these individuals and their significant others.

Currently, it is almost impossible to effectively treat SUD issues as an isolated problem because of the interaction with *intrapersonal, interpersonal,* and *societal* issues. *Intrapersonally,* the SUD may be in response to a trauma experienced before its onset (e.g., physical abuse, sexual abuse, dysfunctional family dynamics). Also, the disorder may be in response to some other problem: *interpersonal* (e.g., interpersonal violence) or *societal* (e.g., homelessness). Counseling, then, requires a *biopsychosocial* perspective, where the interaction of *bio*logical, *psycho*logical, and *social* factors in the individual and their significant others are examined. A biopsychosocial perspective can assist the counselor in addressing issues related to the maintenance of the disorder, thereby enhancing the effectiveness of SUD treatment.

Accurate, research-based knowledge of the dynamics of the disorder is needed to provide effective SUD counseling. Currently, counselors may practice counseling on a continuum, where at one extreme is the grassroots (self-help) emphasis and at the other is the abstract research emphasis. The positive contribution of the grassroots emphasis is that the SUD counseling field essentially evolved out of a grassroots network that is still alive today through self-help groups and peer recovery approaches based on abstinence where recovering individuals help others into recovery. The caution with the grassroots approach is that counselors may be exposed to myths about the disorder that are not anchored in clinical research and then unknowingly (with the best intentions) apply such myths to their clinical practice. The caution at the other end of the continuum is that counselors who are exposed to research findings on SUD may not know how to apply or integrate these findings into their clinical work.

These concerns regarding the training of counselors in the SUD field led to publishing my textbook with Wiley, *Learning the Language of Addiction Counseling* (5th edition) in 2021. This textbook is one of the few books attempting to find a balance between the grassroots emphasis and the abstract research emphasis, resulting in a research-based clinical application approach to SUD counseling. Counselors require practical guidelines and suggestions that stem from a theoretical and research-based knowledge base so that they do not inadvertently enable individuals caught in an active SUD or enable their significant others to directly or indirectly facilitate the presence of the SUD. The fifth edition of *Learning the Language of Addiction Counseling* presents knowledge that is current, emerges from a biopsychosocial perspective, and is in a user-friendly, practical application format (case examples and exercises), facilitating the integration of knowledge into practice by counselors or counselors-in-training. The book, then, is being used by students and practitioners in the mental health field.

This book, *Group Exercises for Substance Use Disorders* (2nd edition), is meant to complement *Learning the Language of Addiction Counseling* (5th edition) (2021). In *Learning the Language of Addiction Counseling* (5th edition) (2021), the fifth chapter of the book, "The Core Treatment Process of Addictions," has a section on group counseling that describes group types, stages of development, techniques, issues, and therapist self-care, as well as a case study and 11 exercises. This section of the book is helpful to readers because it provides an overview of the basic concepts of group work and some group techniques. However, because the textbook does not focus on group techniques, there is limited information available to counselors on specific group techniques that have been helpful in working with SUD clients. A book was needed in addition to the textbook to assist counselors in treating clients with this disorder. The rationale for the book is as follows.

Group therapy is commonly used in SUD treatment centers in the United States (Capuzzi & Gross, 1992; Generes, 2024; SAMHSA, 2021a). It is sometimes seen as the *preferred treatment approach* with addicted clients, because they can learn about themselves interpersonally through their interaction with other group members and learn how to set up a community of support, which is so critical for their recovery (Generes, 2024; Haddock & Sheperts, 2020; Kinney, 2003; Miller, 2024). Also, group therapy is often used in treatment because of its *cost-effectiveness* (Malhotra et al., 2024; Miller, 2021): More individuals can be treated in a short period of time by one or two therapists than that is possible through individual work. This cost effectiveness is appealing to organizations that, because of mental health funding cuts in the current economic times, have the need to operate as efficiently as possible. Finally, SUD treatment has had a *historical record* of using group treatment in working with clients and their loved ones who struggle with this disorder because of both the effectiveness of the treatment and the community of support for recovery (Margolis & Zweben, 1998; O'Leary Tevyaw & Monti, 2022).

A book of group exercises specifically designed for the SUD population is needed for several reasons. *First*, many counselors are being asked to facilitate groups focused on this disorder even though they may have limited experience in the field of SUD counseling. *Second*, many experienced SUD counselors are leaving the field as a result of retirement or in response to current budget cuts, thereby taking their clinical knowledge base with them and leaving neophyte counselors to work with limited mentoring in the SUD counseling field.

In regard to both the first and second reasons, it is natural and normal for counselors to have biases about SUD clients. If they had opportunity to process these biases (e.g., time, experienced SUD counselors to consult), they would be better able to reduce the impact of such biases and enhance the welfare of the SUD client. However, due to limitations on their time and energy, there may be both personal and professional disincentives to address their limited experience and biases. For example, counselors may know that the SUD is a disease, but because of their biases stemming from personal and/or professional experiences with SUD persons, they may send nonverbal or verbal messages that contain a moral judgment or hopelessness for recovery. In a second example of bias, the SUD-related behavior can complicate the view of the SUD as a disease because of its increased frequency, intensity, and focused harm directed to others—result of behaviors told to counselors by SUD patients and/or their family members.

Finally, counselors are increasingly asked to "hit the ground running," so they do not have time to develop group exercises of their own and additionally are often asked to run several treatment groups per week that require them to use different exercises in their groups. They are under great stress in the workplace with their clients, co-workers, and organizations (e.g., paperwork) in addition to their personal stress and experience great technology demands where increased forms of technology are used in both their professional and personal communication.

Clients can respond to the three reasons for this book listed previously by relying on sources of information that can be trusted because the organizations base their information on research as well as clinical experience. I recommend the following organizations for counselors who want accurate, trustworthy information about SUDs:

- National Institute on Alcohol Abuse and Alcoholism (NIAAA)
  www.niaaa.nih.gov

- National Institute on Drug Abuse (NIDA)
  www.drugabuse.gov

- Substance Abuse and Mental Health Services Administration (SAMHSA)
  www.samhsa.gov
  Note that this organization has numerous educational resources regarding prevention of SUD.

I also encourage counselors to contact 12-step self-help referral sites for information because many of their SUD clients, as well as their significant others, may need to rely on such groups for additional support as they recover from the SUD. While I list numerous self-help groups available to clients in *Learning the Language of Addiction Counseling* (5th edition) (Miller, 2021), one example of such groups is AA whose website is www.aa.org and Al-Anon at www.al-anon.org.

The *group exercises in this book* are tried and true by counselors working in the field of SUD counseling. They *originally resulted from trainings* I provided to experienced SUD group counselors at institutes held once or twice a year with 20–40 participants beginning in 1999 and continuing for many years. During trainings, experienced practitioners described one *favorite group counseling technique* that they used with various clients in terms of gender, ethnicity, age, and so on, depending on their clinical population. A portion of these numerous exercises were chosen for this book and rewritten to make them more useful for counselors working in various settings. *For this second edition,* I used *numerous consultants,* as noted in the acknowledgement section, who worked with me over a two-year period of time. These consultants, who had used the first edition of this book in their online, in-person, and/or hybrid groups, provided me with feedback on making the exercises more applicable to the range of group formats in which they work (e.g., online, in-person, and/or hybrid) as well as provided me with feedback on how these exercises could be made more sensitive to diversity. Finally, new exercises were added that were used by some of these consultants in their groups in order to provide me with feedback on their effectiveness. As a result, this book is a collection of powerful exercises used by experienced counselors that can be adapted to a counselor's own practice.

In addition, readers of this text are encouraged to shape these exercises in a manner that fits their population. Because the main concern of our work is the welfare of the client, counselors need to shift exercises to fit the needs of the group (including the format of the group) and the population being served. For example, homework assignments are not noted with the exercises because the counselor, setting (including the format of the group), and/or group members may not be a good match for homework. However, the leader may choose to involve homework with an exercise by adapting it to the group.

This adaptability extends to the materials included in the exercises. Because counselors now work in a variety of group formats (e.g., online, in-person, and/or hybrid), the exercises in this book are primarily process exercises requiring minimal materials that are typically available in an office/practice or an SUD client's home (e.g., paper, pens). For example, in an in-person group, any specific, unique materials (e.g., hula hoops) can be substituted with materials that are readily available (e.g., chairs) in the context of the group format. In order to encourage such flexibility, this book does not have descriptions of materials required for the exercises, because counselors can change all of the materials needed for the exercise to meet the needs and interests of the population being served as well as the group format (e.g., online, in-person, and/or hybrid).

I wanted this book to be easily accessible for busy clinicians who simply want to "pull something off the shelf" in order to do something different in their next group session. Therefore, there are no lengthy sections on goals, objectives, conclusions, processing questions, stages of the group, and so on that one might find in other books. When I buy books on group counseling, I typically do not read those sections; instead, I immediately look at the exercises to determine if I can use them in a group context and carefully read those sections. I made a choice to keep the exercises short because I wanted the book to be user-friendly to busy clinicians who probably do not have time to read a lot about the group application but who want to use exercises that have been used effectively before with SUD clients and their family members/significant others. Nonetheless, in the second section of this book, I include some of my philosophy of group work, with general suggestions and cautions as related to the field of SUD counseling, in order to provide readers with a general framework on my perspective of group work.

Additionally, in each exercise, I have fused methods and directions so that the book reads more like a recipe book. Metaphorically, then, the counselor is the cook: Explicit directions on how to boil water and the like are not being given, but the how-to on combining the components are provided. This book will not meet the need for group work training, although there is a general section describing my approach. I am assuming that readers have had training in group work, and these exercises serve to augment that training. Ideally, readers will have also had training in group work in the SUD field because of the unique flavor that the disorder brings to the application of group counseling. If readers do not have general training or SUD-specific training in group work, you are encouraged to obtain that training, because one can be an effective counselor in general, but it is very important to understand how group counseling operates, so clients (as well as counselors) are not hurt in the powerful process of group counseling. Finally, these exercises can be helpful with clients who struggle with co-occurring disorders as well as mental health clients in general—the adaptation of the exercises to the needs of the client is only limited by the creativity of the counselor. That is why it is critical for counselors to feel the freedom to change the exercises to fit the needs of the client.

Group Exercises for Substance Use Disorders (2nd edition) is designed for prospective and practicing counselors who work with SUD individuals in a group setting. Several broad purposes guided the development of this book on SUD:

1. To provide counseling group techniques to counselors in a language that is easy to understand and readily usable.
2. To provide counseling group techniques to counselors in a format that is easy to access.
3. To assist in the treatment of issues related to the disorder by providing tried-and-true group counseling techniques that address common issues counselors frequently need to address with their clients.
4. To encourage the use of techniques that enhance client awareness of stressors related to the disorder and how to cope with those stressors.
5. To provide a basic group counseling book that can be used in many different treatment settings addressing the disorder.

The categories in Section 3 of the book have been rearranged for the second edition in terms of the current counseling formats counselors need to use in their practice: in-person only, online only, and in-person/online. Note that hybrid groups are not included in the reorganization because the counselor can blend the in-person and the online techniques in order to work in this format. Also, the counselor may find the rearrangement helpful in choosing and processing group exercises that match the group development stages discussed in Section 2 of the book since the counseling format may impact the therapeutic process with regard to the SUD and issues related to their SUD.

I genuinely wish you the very best in this important work with SUD clients. You are helping these clients whose struggles are best summarized in a quote from F. Scott Fitzgerald: "*...in a real dark night of the soul it is always three o'clock in the morning, day after day.*" F. Scott Fitzgerald, The Crack-Up (2009) (p. 75), New Directions. In your work, you can help them with their SUD that takes them to the "dark night of their soul" by welcoming them and inviting hope in them and staying with them on their journey of recovery.

REFERENCES

Adams, W. W. (2025). A wellness deeper than all wounds: Contemplative results for healing from treatment. *The Humanist Psychologist 53* (1): 1–22. https://doi.org/10.1037/hum0000351

American Music Therapy Association, Inc. (AMTA) (2021). *Music therapy and addiction treatment*, 1–3. www.musictherapy.org

Capuzzi, D. & Gross, D. R. (1992). *Introduction to group counseling.* Love.

Generes, W. R. (2024). *Group therapy vs. individual therapy: Uses, benefits, & effectiveness.* American Addiction Centers. https://americanaddictioncenters.org/therapy-treatment/group-individual

Global Council on Brain Health (2020). *Music on our minds: The rich potential of music to promote brain health and mental well-being.* www.GlobalCouncilOnBrainHealth.org; https://doi.org/10.26419/pia.00103.001

Gramlich, J. (2022). *Recent surge in U.S. drug overdose deaths has hit black men the hardest.* Pew Research Center. https://www.pewresearch.org/short-reads/2022/01/19/recent-surge-in-u-s-drug-overdose-deaths-has-hit-black-men-the-hardest/

Greene, D. (2021). Yoga: A holistic approach to addiction treatment and recovery. *OBM Integrative and Complimentary Medicine 6* (4): 1–8.

Haddock, L. R. & Sheperts, D. S. (2020). Chapter 10: Group counseling for treatment in addictions. In D. Capuzzi & M. D. Stauffer (Eds.), *Foundations of addictions counseling* (4th ed., pp. 208–230). Pearson.

Kinney, J. (2003). *Loosening the grip.* McGraw-Hill.

Malhotra, A., Mars, J. A., & Baker, J. (2024). *Group therapy.* National Institutes of Health (NIH). https://www.ncbi.nlm.nih.gov/books/NBK549812/

Margolis, R. D. & Zweben, J. E. (1998). *Treating patients with alcohol and other drug problems: An integrated approach.* American Psychological Association.

Mehegan, L. & Rainville, C. (2020). *AARP music and brain health survey.* Washington, DC: AARP Research. https://doi.org/10.26419/res.00387.001

Miller, G. (2021). *Learning the language of addiction counseling,* (5th ed.). Wiley.

Miller, G. (2024, October). Substance use disorder (SUD) group counseling & group community building: Motivational interviewing focus-Part 2. *Workshop for Addiction Professionals of North Carolina.*

O'Leary Tevyaw, T. & Monti, P. M. (2022). Substance use disorders. In P. J. Bieling, R. E. McCabe, & M. M. Antony (Eds.), *Cognitive-behavioral therapy in groups* (pp. 301–331). Guilford.

Skalski-Bednarz, S. B. & Toussaint, L. L. (2024). A relational model of state of forgiveness and spirituality and their influence on well-being: A two-wave longitudinal study of women with a sexual assault history. *Psychology of Religion and Spirituality 17* (1): 38–46. https://doi.org/10.1037/rel0000526

Substance Abuse and Mental Health Services Administration (SAMHSA) (2021a). *Group therapy in substance use treatment.* https://library.samhsa.gov/sites/default/files/pep20-02-01-020.pdf

Substance Abuse and Mental Health Services Administration (SAMHSA) (2021b). *Key substance use and mental health indicators in the United States: Results from the 2020 National Survey on Drug Use and Health* (HHS Publication No. PEP21-07-01-003, NSDUH Series H-56). Center for Behavioral Health Statistics and Quality, Substance Abuse and Mental Health Services Administration. https://www.samhsa.gov/data/

Substance Abuse and Mental Health Services Administration (SAMHSA) (2024). *Behavioral health of adolescents across sexual identities: Results from the 2023 National Survey on Drug Use and Health* (SAMHSA Publication No. PEP24-07-028). Center for Behavioral Health Statistics and Quality, Substance Abuse and Mental Health Services Administration. https://www.samhsa.gov/data/report/lgb-adolescent-behavioral-health-2023

Substance Abuse and Mental Health Services Administration (SAMHSA) (2025). *National guidance on essential specialty substance use disorder (SUD) care* (Publication No. PEP25-04-033). Substance Abuse and Mental Health Services Administration. https://library.samhsa.gov

Walsh, D. & Koch, G. (2023, November). Helping clients navigate religious trauma. *Counseling Today 66* (5): 33–37.

Wasson, R. S., Dietrich, K. -M., Munjal, V., & Potts, A. A. (2024). Counseling patients on yoga with cultural humility to improve health equity: A guide for clinicians. *Journal of Health Service Psychology 50* (4): 188–197.

2

Philosophy and Practice of Group Work

PERSONAL REFLECTIONS

Readers may ask a legitimate question when initially being exposed to the addictions counseling field: *Why is group work used so much?* This question deserves a thoughtful, multifaceted answer. *First,* all human beings need to be in community with other human beings—although some of us need bigger communities than others. *Second,* because of this need for community, groups can harm us as well as heal us; group therapy is one place where we can heal from harm that has been done to us by others. *Third,* group therapy provides the opportunity to free ourselves from our patterns by offering chances to be and act different within a community of support. For example, there is a saying, "It is our feelings about feelings that get us in trouble" (e.g., our shame about being angry). This feeling experience is one that is common for substance use disorders (SUD) individuals and their loved ones. These group opportunities to be different within a community of support provide an exit from the "disease of isolation" that has been used to describe SUD. *Fourth,* storytelling by leaders

Group Exercises for Substance Use Disorders Counseling, Second Edition. Geri Miller.
© 2025 John Wiley & Sons, Inc. Published 2025 by John Wiley & Sons, Inc.
Companion website: www.wiley.com/go/miller/sud2e

and members is common in a group and, as a Native American elder once said, "Stories teach us how to live." Group members can hear others' stories of how they live with and recover from addiction because their defenses are down as they listen, and they can vicariously learn through others' stories. Metaphorically, the client is a "boat" caught in their "life's storm" and the group steadies them as a "keel" would helping them steer through the storm as a "rudder" would. *Finally*, in this setting, the counselor is not a "star," but rather models a healthy way of being in the world, draws out members, and encourages cohesiveness through sharing, so a healing community can respond to the wounds of SUD clients and their loved ones.

This section of the book is divided into two main areas. The first is an excerpt from my book, *Learning the Language of Addiction Counseling* (5th ed.) (pp. 131–141), that focuses on group counseling—this excerpt is interspersed with comments updating the material. The excerpt is included in case readers do not have that book and would like to be familiar with my philosophy of group counseling with SUD individuals. It is also included because the second part of this section includes "Words to the Wise," a summary of group counseling that is based on this section of text, which has four areas: Developing an SUD Counseling Group, Handling Stage 2 Confrontations of the Leader, Addressing Specific SUD Issues, and Developing Member Awareness. These areas were chosen because they are core, critical areas in the creation of group counseling that encourages healing from addiction.

Finally, a comment to the reader about my rationale for references is included in this section. References were chosen based on my belief of what would be helpful clinically; that means that references may appear to be outdated and unnecessary; however, I made choices to include references clinically rather than academically.

PHILOSOPHY OF GROUP THERAPY

Group therapy is a common form of therapy used in SUD treatment centers in the United States because it assists members in feeling less alone and helping them do self-evaluations (Capuzzi & Gross, 1992; Generes, 2024; SAMHSA, 2021). Also, it is commonly used due to the roots of the SUD field in Alcoholics Anonymous (AA) and the therapeutic community, both of which use substantial group work to help people change (Margolis & Zweben, 1998). Group therapy is sometimes viewed as a treatment of choice for SUD clients because of the power of groups and the ability for clients to learn about themselves by interacting with others, getting social support and feedback, and receiving hope for change (Generes, 2024; Haddock & Sheperts, 2020; Kinney, 2003; Miller, 2024b). While sources of support are considered important, perceived social support is more strongly related to one's adjustment psychologically than received social support (Zell & Stockus, 2025). Group therapy brings clients together who share the common problem of SUD, thereby helping clients stay vigilant about recovery (Generes, 2024; Miller et al., 2019; Vannicelli, 1995); hear the stories of others in recovery (Miller, 2024b); and change through conversational dialogue with other recovering individuals (Miller, 2024b). The popularity of group therapy may also be in relation to its cost-effectiveness (Malhotra et al., 2024; Miller, 2021).

Furthermore, a common difficulty for SUD individuals is interpersonal problems (Capuzzi & Gross, 1992; Miller, 2021). For this reason, group therapy can be very healing for an SUD person's recovery process (Generes, 2024). As Yalom (1985) & Yalom and Leszcz (2020) state, group therapy is a microcosm of the real world. Therefore, how an SUD client operates in the real world will show up in the group–group counseling "catches us at being ourselves" (Miller, 2024b). For example, this aspect allows clients to work through their issues differently including how their past experiences with their family affects their present interactions with others (Miller, 2021).

Additionally, in terms of relationships, SUD is a disease of isolation (Miller, 2021). In this disease, the SUD client views the substance as the solution to their problems even as the consequences of the SUD are the negative impact on relationships. The consequence of the SUD person's use is the impaired ability to develop and maintain relationships. Therefore, group therapy is a potentially powerful healing oasis where SUD clients can learn how to form and maintain relationships with others (Generes, 2024; Miller, 2021).

Because of the prevalence of group work, it is critical that SUD counselors have a basic understanding of group counseling approaches and techniques (Miller, 2021; SAMHSA, 2021). This section discusses types of groups, group stages, leader techniques, specific issues, and therapist self-care. In addition, specific group exercises that can be used with SUD clients are provided.

Types of Groups

Corey (1995, 2016) discusses different types of counseling groups: educational, vocational, social, and personal. SUD groups may be a combination of educational, social, and personal types of groups with some structured groups focusing on a theme of SUD recovery. For example, the National Institutes of Health (NIH) (2023) states that SUD and mental health diagnoses can occur at the same time even if they do not cause one another and that genetics, stress, and trauma can result in the dual diagnosis; these dual-diagnosis clients can be worked with in a group context (Greanias & Siegel, 2000). Also, group work has been discussed from a Motivational Interviewing perspective (Ingersoll et al., 2002), and this perspective can be used in SUD groups.

Some specific areas to examine in the creation of a group are as follows (Corey, 2004):

1. Type
2. Population
3. Goals
4. Need
5. Rationale
6. Leader/co-leader
7. Screening and selection procedures
8. Pragmatics: number of members, location, length, open or closed
9. Topic and focus
10. Group norms (ground rules)

The leader of an SUD group needs to determine the goal for the group and then look at how to set up norms to encourage the achievement of that goal. These norms should be clearly stated in the pregroup interview. If possible, it is a good idea to interview individuals who are going to join the group before they attend their first session. A 15–20 minute interview can allow the leader time to educate the client about the purpose and norms of the group as well as allow the client to obtain a sense of the leader and the group. In this interview, the client can determine if the group will meet their needs and provide an understanding of the leader and the group members (Vassar, 2019). A balance between safety and risk needs to be discussed with each member, while members need to be encouraged to "do life differently." This means that in the group, they can experiment with other people by being different in the group setting. For example, if the client is normally quiet, the client could work at talking more in the group. This encouragement may assist clients in breaking out of lifelong interactional patterns.

Some authors have specific suggestions for a pregroup interview. In this interview, the SUD professional can determine whether the client is appropriate for the group, hear the client's concerns/hopes, and provide group orientation (Malhotra et al., 2024; Margolis & Zweben, 1998). Vannicelli (1995) suggests that information may need to be given in this pregroup interview for clients who have been exposed to self-help groups without previous exposure to group therapy. These clients need to be educated about differences in the therapy group, such as stricter group norms on time and attendance, clearer boundaries, more accountability, cost, discussion of outside group contacts, discussion of group process, focus on and communication of feelings, and exploration of the past and present.

Many times, however, SUD counselors do not have the luxury of a pregroup interview. In these cases, it is helpful for the leader to make some type of contact with the individual either before or during the group, even if it is as simple as shaking the person's hand and introducing themselves. Even the smallest personal contact can facilitate trust with a new group member and help make the group feel comfortable for the client. If a new member joins a group without a pregroup interview, the other group members can educate that individual to the norms of the group as a part of the group process.

If the counselor does not have the luxury of determining group membership, this issue must be discussed within the work environment since adverse outcomes result from a faulty group leader organization of the group (Malhotra et al., 2024). A counselor may face having someone in the group who is very disruptive to the group process. This issue needs to be discussed with a supervisor to determine a policy for handling this difficulty. The counselor also needs to look at having reasonable expectations for themselves as group leader, the members, and group goals. If the counselor is expected to work with whomever is in the group without previous contact, the counselor may need to simply do the best possible work in the present moment of the group session.

A leader must be careful in setting the tone for the group. One of the important bases of a group is the norms that are established (Malhotra et al., 2024). For instance, the leader needs to make sure that people attend the group, and if they cannot, they must know that it is their responsibility to contact the leader. It is helpful to ask members to attend the group five or six times to get a feel for the average group before deciding whether they like or dislike the group. Group members must know that they cannot be sexual with one another in the group because of how such a relationship would affect the dynamics of the group. They need to understand that if they do want to be involved with another group member, it is best to bring up the issue with the leader, who must then consider separating the individuals into different groups. Group members also need to be told the importance of confidentiality as well as the leader's limitations on enforcing such confidentiality (Malhotra et al., 2024). Margolis & Zweben (1998) provide an example of group rules and expectations (see Table 2.1).

This example of group rules and expectations needs to be adapted to the counselor's group. For example, for item 8 in Table 2.1, counselors need to thoughtfully work with how confidentiality is handled in the context of their specific group, population, setting, etc. as well as with professional restrictions on confidentiality.

If a member leaves the group, the leader should allow the group and member a chance to say good-bye. If a member needs to leave the group and there is not a chance for the group to say good-bye, the leader may ask the member whether they want a statement to be read to the group or, at the very least, allow the group a chance to acknowledge the absence of the member in the next session. For in-person groups, it is also important to make sure that there are enough chairs in the group for everyone, including members who are not present. Even though it may sound odd to have empty chairs in the group for individuals who are not there, it communicates an important message to the group that members are still part of the group, even if they cannot make it to one session. For example, a leader may leave an empty chair in the group for a member who drops out of the group while the group discusses this member leaving the group and then remove the chair once the discussion is complete. This provides a ritual for acknowledging the presence and absence of group members.

Also, for in-person groups, the leader needs to be aware of how different chairs in the group can contribute to group dynamics. If there is an extremely comfortable chair, group members may show "sibling rivalry" over that chair by coming early to group to obtain access to it, claiming it as "my chair," or quietly develop resentment toward another client who tends to occupy the chair. There is no need for all chairs to be the same, but if there are differences among the chairs, the group leader can use these differences to be aware of and comment about the group process metaphorically.

Table 2.1 Group Rules and Expectations

Our groups are one of the most lively and powerful parts of our program, but to keep them working well, we ask certain commitments:

1. Come on time.

2. Do not come intoxicated.

3. Notify your group leader if you will be absent or you know you will be late. Other group members are usually concerned about those missing.

4. Keep the identities of the members in strictest confidence. You can share anything you like about what you experience in the group, but not about others.

5. Be open to looking at yourself and your behavior and to giving and receiving feedback. It is especially important to discuss any alcohol or drug use in the group.

6. Although contact with other group members outside group can be beneficial, please do not become involved in any relationship outside group that would interfere with your ability to be honest and explore issues in the group. Romantic or sexual relationships with other group members [are] an obvious example but not the only type of relationship that can be an impediment.

7. A minimum of 3 months' participation is needed to learn to use the group, more to receive full benefits. Please give 1 month's notice if you plan to terminate your participation in the group.

8. There is a list of group members' names and telephone numbers because we think you are an important support system for one another. This list must be kept strictly confidential.

I give/do not give (circle one) permission to have my name on the group list given to members. (First names only on the list.)

I have read and agree to the above rules and guidelines:

Name: ________________   Date: ______________

Source: Reproduced from Margolis & Zweben (1998) / with permission of American Psychological Association.

A leader needs to decide how to open and close sessions to see whether these actions will reinforce targeted behaviors. The counselor needs to find a way to open and close sessions that is comfortable for themselves and respectful to the group members. The counselor can choose the same types of opening and closing statements or different ones. The counselor may begin each week by saying "Let's go around the room and have each person say one word about how easy or difficult it has been for you to stay sober this week," and end the session by saying "Let's hear from each person, in one sentence, what you learned in group today about staying sober." It is important that the counselor make these choices consciously, because they set a tone for how clients enter and exit the group each session. Corey (2004) provides some excellent suggestions for beginning and ending general group sessions that can easily be translated to SUD specific groups. The use of exercises in the group also needs to be examined. Although exercises can be helpful in providing clients with a framework for the group (thereby reducing their anxiety), they may also reinforce dependency on the leader. A counselor needs to find a balance between overusing and underusing exercises in a group.

The group leader also needs to examine how they own power. This form(s) of power will hinge on factors such as the leader's theoretical framework, personal preference of a power form, job title, and client population. Seven possible forms of power the leader can choose from are as follows:

1. *Coercive*, which is based on *fear*. Failure to comply with the leader results in punishment for the members.
2. *Legitimate*, which is based on *leader position*. The leader has the right to expect that suggestions are followed by group members.
3. *Expert*, which is based on the leader possessing *expertise, skill, and knowledge*. The leader is respected for having these traits.
4. *Reward*, which is based on the leader's *ability to reward others*. The leader will provide positive incentives for client compliance.
5. *Referent*, which is based on the leader's *personality traits*. The leader is liked or admired for their personality.
6. *Information*, which is based on the leader's *access to valuable information*. The information the leader has is wanted or needed.
7. *Connection*, which is based on the leader's *connections with others who are influential or important in terms of the organization* (inside or outside of the organization). Group members want to have the positive aspect of the connections and avoid the negative aspects.

The first five forms of power are from French and Raven (1959), while the last two have been added in subsequent literature. The sixth one is from Raven and Kruglanski (1975), and the seventh one is from Hersey and Blanchard (1982). Leaders may have: (1) more than one form of power they use with a group, (2) a favorite form of power, and/or (3) need to change the form of power they typically use because of the type of group they are conducting or the membership of the group. The leader must know and consciously use power for the welfare of the client(s) and for one's own self-care as a counselor.

Finally, if a counselor has a co-leader in the group, the dynamics of this relationship can have a powerful effect on the group. The communication between co-leaders must be very honest and open, with issues being addressed between them. If there are communication problems, they will be acted out in a group, just as marital problems in a family are acted out in the children's behavior. The co-leaders become parents in the group, because the group is a recreation of the family of origin (Yalom, 1985; Yalom & Leszcz, 2020). These projections will be strengthened if one co-leader is male and one is female. However, these projections can be present even if the co-leaders' genders are the same. One co-leader will typically be viewed as the stereotypic mother (caring, supportive, nurturing), and the other co-leader will typically be viewed as the stereotypic father (worldly, disciplinary). Leaders can use these projections to assist clients in healing from their family-of-origin issues, but they need to not let any difficulties between them as leaders be acted out with group members. The co-leaders need to discuss how they will deal with differences both inside and outside the group (e.g., How much do we tell the children about our marital problems and how do we tell them?).

Stages of Group Development

Different group theorists frame group development in various stages (Corey, 2016; Tuckman, 1965; Yalom, 1985; Yalom & Leszcz, 2020). The two theorists' group development stages used in this section are Corey's (2016) model and Tuckman's (1965) model because they are often used by experienced counselors in understanding and explaining the development of groups. While both frameworks are presented and explained separately in following sections, the pairing of their stages is presented here.

Corey's (2016) original framework included six group stages. Two of the stages (Pregroup Issues; Postgroup Issues) are not discussed because this author believes it is most helpful for counselors to understand the four stages of group development that occur between the Pregroup Issues Stage and the Postgroup Issues Stage. The **four group stages** presented here are: ***Initial Stage—Orientation and Exploration [Stage 1]; Transition Stage—Dealing with Resistance [Stage 2]; Working Stage—Cohesion and Productivity [Stage 3]; and Final Stage—Consolidation and Termination [Stage 4].*** Note that these stages have been renumbered by this author because of the omission of two of Corey's stages. Also, to enhance learning, these 4 stages of group development are depicted in corresponding stage development *cartoon graphic panels* in an entertaining, educational manner using animals in a group setting. The panels are incorporated as follows: (1) in the *hard copy text version* of this book, the panels are in black and white; (2) in the *electronic text version* of this book, the panels are in color; and (3) in both *hard copy and electronic versions*, the panels are available in color in the Teacher Resources section accompanying this book.

Originally **Tuckman (1965)** presented **four group stages** [*"Forming"; "Storming"; "Norming"; "Performing"*] (Egolf, 2001) and in approximately 1975 added **stage five** to the original model [*"Adjourning"*] (Ibrahim, 2021). Tuckman's group stages are typically known by counselors as the labels in quotation marks (Ibrahim, 2021; Malhotra et al., 2024). For that reason, this author pairs Corey's group stages with the typical terminology used by counselors for Tuckman's group stages as follows:

> **Stage 1:** ***Initial Stage—Orientation and Exploration*** (Corey, 2016); ***"Forming"*** (Tuckman, 1965);
>
> **Stage 2:** ***Transition Stage—Dealing with Resistance*** (Corey, 2016); ***"Storming"*** (Tuckman, 1965);
>
> **Stage 3:** ***Working Stage—Cohesion and Productivity*** (Corey, 2016); ***"Norming/Performing"*** (Tuckman, 1965); and
>
> **Stage 4:** ***Final Stage—Consolidation and Termination***; ***"Adjourning"*** (Tuckman, 1975 as cited in Ibrahim, 2021).

Note that Stage 3 of Corey's group development stages incorporates two of Tuckman's group development stages. Also, Tuckman's 1975 additional stage of "adjourning" (Tuckman, 1975 as cited in Ibrahim, 2021) is paired with Stage 4 of Corey's group development stages.

There has also been an inclusion of metaphorical stages of group development developed by the author that may assist the reader in remembering the stages of group development. This inclusion follows the explanation of the group development stages according to Corey (2016) and Tuckman (1965; 1975 as cited in Ibrahim 2021).

The counselor needs to remember that these group stages are not fixed or clear-cut. Groups may show evidence of going back and forth between the stages, depending on membership changes in the group or issues that arise in the group. Also, when group membership changes for each session, the group leader may need to look at each session as one where each of these stages is touched on in that session. Thus, although there may not be a carryover from session to session in terms of group development, it primarily occurs in each session because the group is so significantly changed in terms of membership each time. This perspective can reflect the approach advocated earlier, where the group leader has expectations that are reasonable given the context of the group.

Stage 1: Initial Stage—Orientation and Exploration (Corey, 2016)

The first stage of group development is what may be called the "cocktail party" stage, where members are nervous about attending the group. During this stage, members generally are involved in superficial chitchat that does not reveal much about themselves.

As Corey's (2016) title (Orientation and Exploration) implies, members are trying to orient themselves to the group and explore how they are expected to function within the group. A central issue for members is the theme of trust (Corey, 2016). As members are determining group rules and norms, they are also trying to determine a sense of whether they belong in this group and whether they will be accepted by the other group members as well as by the group leader.

SUD clients may show these initial group development behaviors in specific ways. For example, superficial chitchat may be "junkie of the year" competition bragging. Here, a client may talk with other clients about how many different types of drugs they have used, how much of certain drugs has been taken, or how many consequences have been experienced, such as DUIs (Driving Under the Influence). This information sharing may appear both deep and meaningful, but the client is truly sharing information that, to some degree, is already known by the counselor and other individuals in the client's life. This chitchat may serve as a distraction from the painful issues in the client's life that led to or resulted from the SUD. At the same time, this information is important for the client to share to determine how similar or dissimilar they are to other group members and to determine whether these members will be judgmental. The group leader, then, who should be aware of the need for such information to be shared by members, also needs to monitor whether this information sharing is an avoidance technique being used by the clients. If it appears to be an avoidance technique, the counselor will need to set limits on this type of sharing and encourage group members to share at a more personal level.

Stage 1: "Forming" (Tuckman, 1965)

In this stage, there is a positive interpersonal climate where affability and friendliness are prevalent; however, this is a superficial climate because members are determining factors such as who will lead, follow, cooperate, challenge (e.g., try to control) the group (Egolf, 2001; Malhotra et al., 2024).

The group depends on the leader for guidance and direction asking questions about the group and ground rules that are set (Ibrahim, 2021; Malhotra et al., 2024; Tuckman, 1965). Members are polite, hesitant about joining, avoid conflict, want to feel safe and approved of, and discuss topics not relevant to the group (Ibrahim, 2021; Malhotra et al., 2024; Tuckman, 1965). They may feel excited and/or anxious, concerned about expectations, and uncertain about the group (Ibrahim, 2021; Malhotra et al., 2024; Tuckman, 1965).

Stage 1: "Birth/Trust" (Miller, 2024b)

In Stage 1, the metaphor used for this stage is "Birth/Trust." The group is essentially being "born" and like at the birth of a human being, they do not understand what is happening to them. For example, they are overwhelmed by the stimuli they are experiencing and do not feel safe, are unsure who to trust (e.g., leader; group members), how much to trust, and look to the parent (e.g., leader to protect them and tell them what to do).

Initial stage: orientation and exploration
Welcome to our group. Please introduce yourself and tell us what substance you have abused the most.
Name is Cat, I struggle with acid.
My name is Elephant I struggle with gambling
My name is Dog, I struggle with pot.
My name is Panda i struggle with fentanyl
My name is Racoon, i struggle with metamphetamine.
My name is Wolf, i struggle with alcohol
My name is Bunny, I struggle with Xanax.

Stage 2: Transition Stage—Dealing with Reluctance
(Corey, 2016)

Stage 2 of group development is often a difficult stage for both clients and the leader. In this stage of group development, the leadership of the group is challenged. Prior to this stage, the leader may have looked like an omnipotent parent to members (Yalom, 1985; Yalom & Leszcz, 2020). During Stage 2, members are questioning the leader's ability to direct the group. The members are really trying to find out how safe the group is for them. Knowledge of this level of safety emerges from struggles with power and control. Typically, this challenge is initially directed to the leader, in part to determine how the leader acts when stressed in situations. It is a parallel process to what a person may do in an intimate relationship to find out how safe they are with an individual by fighting with the individual or, staying with the family metaphor, how safe the kids are when the parent(s) is upset. Note that the SUD population, in general, tends to be "button pushers" who can easily bring out negative reactions from others. Counselors, then, need to be aware of this tendency and prepare themselves for a possibly intense challenge when working with the SUD population at this stage of group development (Miller, 2024a).

Once the leader has been challenged, group members will repeat this process with other group members. Group members will not confront one another until the leader is challenged because of the need to see how conflict is addressed in the group. These conflicts will show how the leader responds to conflict and how other members in the group act when they are challenged.

At this stage of development, SUD clients may challenge group leaders in a variety of ways. The leaders, if they are not in SUD recovery, may be asked what they know about SUD and how they dare to work with SUD clients when they have never faced these issues. If leaders are in SUD recovery, they may be challenged by being asked what types of drugs were done or how long they used. Leaders may also be challenged on gender or ethnicity differences, again questioning how well they can understand the struggles of the members. Vannicelli (1995) elaborates on specific challenges to leadership from a 12-step perspective. These challenges include the client's having an overzealousness of AA 12-step programs, being too literal about 12-step philosophy (e.g., "slogan resistance" in which the client uses slogans to avoid addressing personal issues, such as "live in the present" rather than address past issues), using 12-step program terminology in a defensive manner (e.g., "I just have to let go of it"), and using program labels to avoid experiencing conflict or differences (e.g., "alcoholic behavior"). Whatever the form of the challenge, leaders are questioned on their competence. This questioning process reflects the underlying anxiety of the group members and the level of resistance or willingness they have to discuss concerns at a deeper level. Group leaders, while responding to questions directed to them, also need to redirect the focus from themselves by refocusing the group's attention to the underlying anxiety and resistance and processing this anxiety and resistance with the group.

SUD clients often have a poor history with conflict resolution. They frequently come from families or drug use experiences where conflict was "unchecked" and resulted in violence—physically, emotionally, or psychologically. The SUD counselor needs to keep this tendency in mind when working with SUD clients so that the group is a safe place where clients learn that conflict does not mean violence and that they can learn conflict resolution techniques. At this stage, the counselor can use conflict that occurs as a natural part of the group process to teach clients to handle conflict in a different manner. Counselors need to encourage clients to be aware and express their issues with conflict requiring the counselor to watch the verbal and nonverbal behavior of clients during group sessions. Thus, the counselor may need to encourage confrontation from clients to the leader so the counselor can be a role model for how to handle conflict and set norms for how conflict will be handled in this group.

Stage 2: "Storming" (Tuckman, 1965)

In this stage, conflict dominates as a result of anxiety experienced by group members (Egolf, 2001; Malhotra et al., 2024). There is resistance expressed to the leader, and conflict/hostility is expressed by individuals to the leader and other group members (Ibrahim, 2021; Malhotra et al., 2024; Tuckman, 1965). There is vying among members for positions of power in the group (including leadership), and there is a lot of uncertainty in the group that results in factions within the group (Ibrahim, 2021; Malhotra et al., 2024; Tuckman, 1965). Such conflict needs to be "managed" in such a way that the group is able to move on to the next stage of the Tuckman model (1965) where they can establish group norms (Egolf, 2001). The leader may need to help in finding compromises in the group (Ibrahim, 2021).

Stage 2: "Adolescence/Conflict" (Miller, 2024b)

The metaphor used for this stage is "Adolescence/Conflict." Here, the group encourages some of the members, who are more comfortable challenging leaders, to challenge the group leader in order to determine how safe the group is.

These members act as adolescents act in challenging authority—no matter what the parent does, it is not right. The group leader needs to stay calm, as one would with an adolescent, and point out the inconsistencies in what they are asking of the leader. This stage can be discouraging for the leader, as parents of an adolescent experience, but if the leader can stay calm, the members can move on to the next stage. Also, all members of the group will not challenge the leader; some members will be supportive of the leader during this stage.

Stage 3: Working Stage—Cohesion and Productivity (Corey, 2016)

In the working stage of group development, group cohesion has developed, and members trust and feel close to one another. Members share information about themselves on a deep and meaningful level. In the context of the group, they are now willing to look at issues with which they have struggled. Members are comfortable being direct and confrontational with one another. The leader is seen by group members in a more realistic light of having both strengths and weaknesses.

In working with SUD clients at this stage of group development, the leader may find that members are willing to discuss their personal issues in depth, Rather than simply discussing the drugs they have used, they may be willing to discuss the shameful and embarrassing actions they took to obtain drugs. They may discuss how they felt as children growing up in SUD homes. Issues that emerge are discussed with an expression of vulnerability and openness. At this stage, members are willing to be supportive and share their own places of pain with others in the group.

Stage 3: "Norming/Performing" (Tuckman, 1965)

In the norming stage, there is a resolution of conflict and, as a result, there is a development of cohesion due to new standards and roles emerging and members are freer in their interactions developing a "we" sense in the group (Egolf, 2001; Malhotra et al., 2024). Here, in the norming stage, individuals begin to feel as though they are a part of the group and that by acceptance of others, they can make accomplishments in the group (Ibrahim 2021; Malhotra et al., 2024; Tuckman, 1965). Roles and responsibilities, which are clear, are accepted by group members with a strong sense of commitment to and unity within the group (Ibrahim, 2021; Malhotra et al., 2024; Tuckman, 1965). There is a strong sense of belonging and acceptance of one another as well as trust and open communication (Ibrahim, 2021; Malhotra et al., 2024; Tuckman, 1965).

In the performing stage, the group has become cohesive, conforms to the group, and focuses on solving problems (Egolf, 2001; Malhotra et al., 2024; Tuckman, 1965). Also, in the performing stage, the atmosphere is an open one where members feel as though they can trust each other and work together without hierarchy and with flexibility (Ibrahim, 2021; Malhotra et al., 2024; Tuckman, 1965). At this point, the members are strongly connected and do not need much guidance or participation from the leader, and they look after each other understanding strengths and weaknesses of other members as well as group process (Ibrahim, 2021; Malhotra et al., 2024; Tuckman, 1965). The leader still oversees the development of the group (Ibrahim, 2021; Malhotra et al., 2024; Tuckman, 1965).

Stage 3: "Adult/Trust" (Miller, 2024b)

The metaphor used for this stage is "Adult/Trust." In this stage, the group leader takes a "background" role as a parent would do with their children. The group members are tending to each other as adults would, and because of the resolution of Stage 2 issues where they watched how the parent handled challenges, they have taken on the roles that the leader held and are tending to the needs of one another. Like a parent with adult children, the leader is there for support if needed but does not step in and interfere with their lives unless asked or determines that it is necessary for the "child's" safety or well-being.

Because of the honesty expressed in the previous stage, in this stage of group development, the members share leadership roles previously held by the leader.
The leader allows members to take on the roles while monitoring the group members' interactions and reinforcing how much the group cares about the members who shares their struggle.

Stage 4: Final Stage—Consolidation and Termination (Corey, 2016)

In the final stage of group development, members are facing issues of termination and attempting to integrate their experiences in the group into their daily lives. Strong feelings about termination may emerge for members, as well as concerns about how well they may apply these group experiences to their lives. Themes of loss and grief may appear. The loss of loved ones through death or through the consequences of their drug use may be present. Feelings of abandonment and betrayal may also emerge. The leader, for example, might be accused of not really caring for the SUD individuals because the group will end, and they will not be able to see the leader again. Also, at this stage, group members are also looking to the future of their lives following the group experience. The leader, as well as assisting them with issues related to termination, also needs to assist them in summarizing what they have learned from the group and how they may use this knowledge and behavior change in the future.

Stage 4: "Adjourning" (Tuckman, 1975)

Around 1975, Tuckman revised his theory of four group stages and added the fifth stage, "Adjourning" that was also called "Deforming" and "Mourning" (Ibrahim, 2021). This stage is not connected with the four stages of group development, but more related to the well-being of group members (Ibrahim, 2021; Malhotra et al., 2024); that is why this stage of Tuckman's is incorporated into Stage 4 of group development where members are taking in the reality that the group is ending and need to be attended to in terms of their personal needs.

Stage 4: "Death/Grief and Loss" (Miller, 2024b)

In this stage, the metaphor used for this stage is "Death/Grief & Loss." Here, the group is living with the reality of the "death" of the group and members are experiencing grief and loss related to the group ending. Previous issues related to death/grief and loss may emerge triggered by the group ending. The leader, like a parent, needs to make sure that the "children" are encouraged to be aware of and express their grief and loss both related to the group (including the loss of the leader) as well as other losses experienced earlier. The leader, as a parent, also needs to guide the "children" to the hope for their future.

Final stage: consolidation and termination
Leader: Say one thing you learned from this group and how you plan to make this behavior change in your life.

I learned a lot from this group about how to handle my anger other than getting drunk. Thank you for helping me.
Thank you for helping me work through my issues with trauma.
Thank you. Goodbye. I will miss you.
I also want to tell you I will miss each of you in this group because you have all cared about each other through hard times.

olive barry- cartoon graphic designer
In the last group of the final stage of group development,
the leader encourages members to share their grief about
the group ending as well as encouraging them to look to
the future by discussing how they will make the
behavior change in their lives outside of the group once it ends.

Table 2.2 Integration Summary of Corey's Stages, Tuckman's Stages, and Miller's Stages

Stages	Corey's Stages	Tuckman's Stages	Miller's Stages
Stage 1	Initial Stage—Orientation and Exploration	"Forming"	"Birth/Trust"
Stage 2	Transition Stage—Dealing with Reluctance	"Storming"	"Adolescence/Conflict"
Stage 3	Working Stage—Cohesion and Productivity	"Norming" "Performing"	"Adult/Trust"
Stage 4	Final Stage—Consolidation and Termination	"Adjourning"	"Death/Grief and Loss"

Table 2.2 has been included to assist the reader in summarizing the integration of Corey (2016), Tuckman (1965; 1975), and Miller (2024) group stages.

At this time, it is difficult to determine how telehealth may impact the group development stages. However, the counselor can use the following self-reflective questions to explore, possibly with a supervisor/mentor/colleague, the impact of telehealth on group development (Miller, 2024b):

1. At *Stage 1*, do members have increased anxiety?
2. Are there fewer or more challenges at *Stage 2*?
3. Does the counselor need to increase their effort in order to encourage vulnerable sharing at *Stage 3*?
4. In *Stage 4*, are there difficulties for clients and leaders when graduating is not face-to-face?

Group Leader Techniques

Group leaders can facilitate the transitions in the stages of group development by acknowledging the need for certain factors to be present and by encouraging the presence of those factors in the group. Because two of Yalom's (Yalom, 1985)

11 therapeutic factors for group development—installation of hope and universality—seem especially related to the issues of addicted clients, they are discussed here.

Installation of hope is a very powerful tool in working with addicted clients. These individuals may have previously tried to address their addiction and found themselves back in it despite their best efforts. If a leader can communicate hope to clients, this hope may assist them in making important changes in their lives. The leader's belief in the client's ability to change may assist with the client's motivation level, as well as provide the client with support to make changes around addictive behavior. For example, the leader can simply encourage clients to "do it differently" in the context of the group—that is, to try different behaviors in an attempt to achieve and maintain sobriety.

This experience can lead to what Yalom (1985) calls the corrective emotional experience:

> The client heals from a previous trauma by re-experiencing the emotions in the group and having a chance to reflect on them. For example, a client may have let down many people in attempts to be sober and, as a result, has been ostracized from significant others because of the addictive behavior. If a client relapses in a group and has the experience to process feelings and thoughts about the relapse within an honest, caring, supportive group that holds the client responsible for the relapse behavior, the client may experience hope about staying sober. In addition, the client has the corrective emotional experience of still being cared for and supported by the group to make another attempt at recovery.

Universality is the sense that the individual is not unique in his or her problems or situations (Yalom, 1985; Yalom & Leszcz, 2020). This sense can reduce a feeling of social isolation for the addicted individual. One way for this sense to be encouraged is for the therapist to work in the here and now. In other words, the therapist is aware of what is happening in the group at the present moment and watches for items of similarity among members. Commenting on such similarities can assist with the sense of universality, which can provide a strong basis for the group to explore specific issues related to addictions because of the experiences they have in common. In addition, the experience of universality can be healing in and of itself because of the tendency for SUD individuals to be isolated from others as a result of their SUD and related behaviors. The universality can provide the client with the sense of belonging to a community. For example, a client who has had extramarital affairs related to their use may have been isolated from their partner, children, church members, neighbors, and friends, who thought the affairs were a statement on what a bad person the SUD person is. Coming to a group and hearing how others made the mistake of having extramarital affairs may be healing for the SUD client and encouraging for them to discuss other issues related to dependency.

Leaders may find some other group techniques helpful when working with SUD clients. Connors et al. (2015) state that while the history of substance abuse treatment has been confrontational in style in order to break the client's denial about substance abuse problems, such a style can result in client resistance or treatment dropouts. Rather, the authors advocate a supportive, empathic, client-centered style that invites clients to change. In general, group leaders need to listen actively; reflect meaningfully; facilitate goal achievement; and clarify, summarize, empathize, interpret, question, confront, support, diagnose, evaluate, and terminate appropriately within the group context.

Finally, group leaders need to use techniques that are a good match with the characteristics of the SUD clients with whom they work (Capuzzi & Gross, 1992). Leaders need to be directive by being focused and disciplined, which is important for SUD clients who may have low frustration tolerance and impulsiveness. They also need to confront both indirectly and directly to help clients break self-defeating patterns.

Leaders must also be tolerant toward emotionalism expressed by members and nondefensive, especially concerning anger and hostility. By being directive, respectfully confrontive, tolerant, and nondefensive, leaders can assist groups in becoming more cohesive as well as provide SUD clients with role-modeling behaviors that are helpful to their recovery process.

Specific Issues

While relapse may or may not occur, the counselor needs to be prepared to address this possibility when working with SUD individuals in a group setting. For example, each leader needs to think about the conditions under which individuals who relapse will be allowed to remain in the group (Capuzzi & Gross, 1992; Miller, 2021). Also, the counselor needs to determine how to assist

SUD clients in decreasing the chances of substance use through awareness of high-risk situations and use of problem-solving strategies (SAMHSA, 2005). For example, simple approaches such as encouraging mindfulness through 12-step slogans (e.g., "One day at a time"; "First things first"; "Easy does it") or imagining oneself using and what occurs (e.g., "Follow the drink/drug through") can be helpful for clients in terms of relapse prevention (Miller, 2024b). The hope is to assist them in finding a balanced lifestyle that discourages relapse (Miller, 2024a).

There is a thin line between compassion for how difficult it is to change a habit and encouraging the addicted individual to continue using (Miller, 2021). Relapse is understandable if an individual has a commitment to sobriety and is willing to learn from the relapse by exploring it in the group therapy context, as well as possibly individually with the therapist (Miller et al., 1995; Miller, 2021). No matter what the client's commitment to sobriety is, the SUD is a difficult disease to recover from and counselors need to assist clients in determining what the barriers are to their sobriety and address the relapse in a matter-of-fact manner (Miller, 2024a).

It is important that group members accept consequences for their relapses—the counselor needs to have compassion for the SUD client's story of their relapse while holding them accountable for their behavior (*compassionate accountability*) (Miller, 2024a). It is best that these consequences be clearly outlined in the group before the relapse occurs. For example, the counselor in the pregroup interview tells each recovering client that he or she is expected to remain sober, but if a relapse occurs, the client must let the counselor know of the relapse. This relapse would then be discussed openly in the group to determine what needs to be done differently to help the client stay sober. The client must understand that relapse does not automatically mean dismissal from the group (assuming the counselor is able to make such a promise) but that repeated relapses mean that the client's recovery is not working, and treatment alternatives may need to be explored with the counselor as well as the group.

Alfonso (2023) and Vannicelli (1995) also caution group leaders about the issues of countertransference regarding substances. Alfonso (2023) states that countertransference in clients can result in the counselor feeling hopeless, embarrassed, and wrong. Vannicelli (1995) provides specific cautions to counselors in recovery: (1) remember their role is different from a 12-step meeting, especially in terms of client welfare; (2) address the smell of alcohol in a group openly, even if uncertain as to who has been drinking; and (3) negotiate recovery contracts so they are supportive rather than automatic or formula based. Vannicelli's (1995) second comment can be adapted to online groups by counselors monitoring the verbal and nonverbal behavior of members.

Typically, SUD clients have problems with authority figures, trusting others, emotional reactivity, and impulse control. Problems with authority figures are discussed in the section on therapist self-care. The other three themes, which need to be monitored throughout the group development stages, are discussed briefly here. Because trust of others may be a serious issue, the group leader needs to work hard at encouraging individuals to be both honest and respectful toward one another throughout the group sessions. An atmosphere of such honesty will assist members in trusting one another. At the same time, group members need to learn to work with their emotional reactivity and their poor impulse control. They must be encouraged to listen to their emotions and their impulses but to delay acting on them until they have seriously anticipated the consequences of their behavior. Thus, clients learn to recognize and express their emotions in ways that are honest and respectful toward others.

Two areas that may pose problems in a group with addicted individuals are denial and resistance (Capuzzi & Gross, 1992). Denial needs to be viewed as a component of the SUD (Yamashita et al., 2021). Group members who have denial need to be confronted on the discrepancies of their behaviors, thoughts, and feelings. This does not have to be a highly emotional confrontation; in fact, a calm, neutral approach may help the client hear the confrontation less defensively, but the confrontation needs to be anchored in behavior. If possible, it is highly effective to have members confront one another on the presence of denial or resistance. Again, however, such confrontation, while honest, also needs to be respectful and caring. The counselor should note, however, that resistance in an SUD individual may be healthy in that the client may be aware that they lack adequate support to address such issues. The client may not be willing to look at specific issues at that time because they do not have the necessary resources internally or externally to address them. In such a case, the counselor may encourage the client to state this limitation to the group and work with the client on building internal and external supports that would allow for such issues to be addressed.

Therapist Self-Care

One of the main areas that will assist a group in developing is this ability of the therapist to work with the group's transference on their leadership role (characteristics projected onto the leader). As Yalom (Yalom, 1985; Yalom & Leszcz, 2020) states, the leader must remember that the transference is connected to the role. At the same time, the leader also needs to be aware that struggles with the leadership will be shaped by the traits/style of the leader.

These projections are examined in terms of self-care overall and group development stages specifically in relation to self-care practices of the leader. In terms of *self-care*, counselors need to:

1. remember they do not need to know everything;
2. honor their own "wounds" (e.g., places of personal vulnerability especially related to SUD);
3. focus on making progress with working with the SUD population and not needing to do the work perfectly; and
4. practice self-care by: (1) avoiding being **Hungry**, **Angry**, **Lonely**, **Tired** (**HALT**) prior to working with the SUD population; (2) knowing one's own limits in working with this population; (3) being **Honest**, **Open**, and **Willing** (**HOW**) in one's work with this population; and (4) having a routine of practicing self-care regularly by meeting one's needs in terms of diet, exercise, sleep, and mind/emotions/spirit (Miller, 2024a).

Group development stages specifically in relation to self-care practices of the leader are as follows:

During the *first stage of group development*, the leader is closely watched by group members. When the leader enters the room (in-person) or begins the group (virtual), the members might become very quiet, and during discussions, members may turn often to the leader for feedback and suggestions. Group leaders will likely react differently to this focus of attention. For some, it may be uncomfortable to be under the magnifying glass of the group. These leaders may need to learn how to relax and be themselves when in the spotlight. Others who like to have the spotlight and be seen as having all the answers may need to proceed cautiously with feedback to members. In short, these leaders need to keep their egos in check for the sake of the group development and encourage members to be responsible for themselves.

The primary goal for the leader in the first stage of group development is to help the members feel comfortable in the group by making the group an inviting place for them to attend. The leader should allow members to have superficial conversations while also inviting them to look at deeper issues. The leader must closely monitor their own behavior, so the norms being set for the group are the ones the counselor wants to have set.

During the *second stage of group development*, the leader encourages criticism from the group members. Here, the leader is monitoring for verbal and nonverbal signs of disagreement with the leadership. It is important for the leader to facilitate such challenges, so that the group members learn how to confront one another in the group and learn that they are safe even if they challenge the authority structure of the group.

The counselor knows that it is impossible to please all members of the group at this stage. Like the parent of an adolescent, whatever action they take, the group members will find some fault with it. If the therapist is caring, the group members may say that they want more authority. If the counselor is authoritative, the group members may say that they want more flexibility. The group attack on the leadership will never be unanimous (Yalom, 1985; Yalom & Leszcz, 2020), but to some degree, it will be personal.

The leader must acknowledge their flaws and possibly apologize to the group. The group will be closely watching the leader to see how they deal with being confronted. By remembering that the members are transferring their projections from previous experiences with authority figures, the leader will be less likely to be overwhelmed by the experience. It may also help to remember that allowing the group the process of challenging the leadership is exactly what will help the group move into the working stage. Thus, it is necessary for the counselor to learn how to take on the group's criticism. They must model an openness to feedback and find a way to ground themselves during the challenge.

This process of anchoring may vary among group leaders. Some may find it helpful to take a deep breath before responding to criticism. Others might place both feet on the floor and uncross their arms while doing a visualization that they are connected to the earth and that they will survive this confrontation. Whatever means of self-care is practiced by the leader, it is imperative that they not strike back at the group member(s) who is doing the challenging. They must realize that the individual is simply the mouthpiece of the challenge for the group—the one individual speaking is also speaking for others. The counselor, then, needs to encourage other members to speak their dissatisfaction with the leadership so that one individual does not monopolize the group and run the danger of becoming a scapegoat in the group.

Because many SUD clients have had negative experiences with authority figures, Stage 2 is critical in an SUD group. The leader needs to firmly guide the group through this stage of development by being honest, open, and willing to work through the challenge. Becoming resistive or defensive can stop the group at this stage of development.

During *Stage 3 of group development*, the leader turns over different leadership functions, such as beginning and ending the group, establishing the focus of the group session, or, for in-person groups, maintaining the physical aspects of the group space (e.g., chair arrangement, room temperature). This turning over the leadership functions may be difficult for leaders who have a high need for control, but it is important for the group members, who have grown in their sense of autonomy. Self-care at this stage means that the group leader needs to be sensitive to their own reactions to not being "center stage," but having more of the "on-call" stance in relation to the group.

During *Stage 4 of group development*, the leader must be comfortable with issues of death and loss. The leader needs to help members process their own grief reactions to the group ending as well as allow themselves a chance to grieve about the ending of the group. An important part of self-care as a leader is allowing self some supports in being a therapist during this stage. The support and feedback of trusted colleagues, a supervisor, or a mentor will assist the counselor working in this stage.

WORDS TO THE WISE*

* If the reader does not feel confident or competent to ensure that transgender and/or nonbinary clients are included and protected in a group setting, the counselor may want to consider obtaining consultation, support, and/or continuing education to assist in providing counseling that promotes the welfare of the client. This recommendation pertains to: formation of the group, stages of group development, and choice/adaptation of exercises. Specifically, in Stage 2 of group development, the reader may want to seek support and consultation with professionals who have had experience in working with transgender and/or nonbinary clients in order to be supportive of them during this stage.

In terms of exercises, during introductions, the counselor needs to consider how to model the preference of pronouns for this population and consider how they may protect this population if they face hostility from other group members. The counselor's goals with this population need to be: welcoming them, ensuring their safety, and supporting them while not isolating them.

Developing an SUD Counseling Group

1. Think of group development as **taking on a project**, such as building something, planting a garden, or cooking a meal. Do this even if you have limited choice about the creation of the group. Focus on those aspects of the group where you do have a choice. Once you have this perspective in mind, ask yourself questions about the type of group you want to create in terms of:

   a. Type
   b. Population
   c. Goals
   d. Need
   e. Rationale
   f. Leader/co-leader
   g. Screening and selection procedures
   h. Pragmatics: number of members, location, length, open versus closed
   i. Topic and focus
   j. Group norms (ground rules)

2. **Know the stages of group development** in terms of your theoretical framework. Use that framework to guide your orientation in approaching each group session as well as techniques you choose to facilitate group development.

3. With regard to **exercise choice**, choose an exercise that matches the stage of group development of your group. Then remember four main guidelines. First, before using the exercise in the group, process its use with a supervisor, mentor, or colleague, have someone supervise your implementation of the exercise, and/or try it out on yourself first so you do not go in cold to the group with a new exercise. Second, when choosing an exercise to use in a group, multiply the time you anticipate by at least two so neither you nor group members feel rushed in the process; another exercise can always be added if there is time remaining in the group.

Third, always have a backup exercise planned in the event that the one you introduce flops. Fourth, remember that group members can learn by watching others in the group (vicarious learning), so all group members do not need to process their experiences with an exercise at the same level.

4. Practice **leader self-care** throughout the group development stages. Be aware that, like a parent, some of us may shine as well as struggle with different development stages. For example, some parents may be exceptional with infants, whereas others do better in the child's adult years. As with parenting, leaders can learn both their strengths and weaknesses so as to enhance development as much as possible. The ongoing practice of self-care can assist the parent/leader in being the best he or she can be with the child/group.

Handling Stage 2 Confrontations of the Leader

1. In general, the leader can practice any of the following **overall approaches** to assist in handling the challenge in a calm, nonjudgmental manner that will facilitate the group evolution into Stage 3:

♦ Breathe
♦ Be calm
♦ Intentionally slow yourself down
♦ Own your power
♦ Use positive, supportive self-talk
♦ Have open, relaxed body language
♦ Detach and look at the process: look for a learning opportunity for clients' learning skills and talk about how conflict is dealt with in group
♦ Don't take the challenge personally
♦ Bring the confrontation into the open and examine it for underlying issues
♦ Listen and be open (nonauthoritarian)
♦ Listen to group member(s)
♦ Reflect what the person is saying in the challenge
♦ Ask the other group members what they think of the challenge
♦ Check it out with the group if other people are experiencing the same reactions
♦ Admit your mistake(s) and apologize if appropriate
♦ Deal with the challenge by focusing on a solution and move on
♦ Help members be comfortable with nonresolution at times

2. The leader may also make **specific statements** that may assist in calming down both self and group members during this stressful time:

  - "What makes you think that's true?"
  - "Thank you for that information. You have taught me some things about myself, and I will take this into consideration."
  - "Tell me more about your dissatisfaction with me as a leader."
  - "What do other group members think of this challenge?"
  - "What does this challenge remind you of, and how did you deal with it?"
  - "What have you learned to do differently as you have challenged me as a leader or observed me being challenged?"

Addressing Specific SUD Issues

1. Note that as a counselor, it is important to explore our own potential **countertransference issues** in working in the area of SUD counseling.
2. Be aware of **specific issues** that commonly arise in working with SUD clients, including:

  - Relapse
  - Authority
  - Trust
  - Emotional reactivity
  - Poor impulse control
  - Letting go (experiencing the powerlessness in living, including the past and loss)
  - Denial
  - Resistance

3. Choose **techniques** for the group that will assist clients with these common issues.
4. Be aware of how these different **issues may emerge uniquely** in the different stages as well as with different populations. Also note that members may vary on the amount and type of issue(s) with which they struggle.

Developing Group Member Awareness

1. Find out **members' beliefs about groups**. Ask what they have seen through different visual mediums (e.g., television, YouTube, movies; podcasts; etc.) and what have they experienced as group members. Such experiences may predispose them to stereotypes about groups that are inaccurate, thereby inhibiting their capacity to learn about themselves and others in the group context.

2. Inform group members about what they can **expect in a counseling group** by providing them with a handout and/or discussion prior to the first group session or during it where they learn:

   a. A definition of group therapy
   b. Why group therapy works
   c. What they can talk about in group therapy (including limits such as confidentiality)
   d. How to participate in the group
   e. The advantages of group therapy in comparison to individual therapy
   f. The atmosphere of group therapy (norms of safety, respect, feedback)
   g. Typical client concerns about group therapy

3. Stress that in group therapy, they have the unique experience of learning about their "blind spots" and discussing their "hidden spots" through a supportive community. This information may encourage their interest and participation in the group.

REFERENCES

Alfonso, C. A. (2023). Clinical implications of countertransference in the treatment of addictions. *Psychodyn Psychiatry, 51,* 133–140. https://pubmed.ncbi.nlm.nih.gov/37260240/

Capuzzi, D., & Gross, D. R. (1992). *Introduction to group counseling.* Love.

Connors, G. J., Donovan, D. M., DiClemente, C. C., & Velasquez, M. M. (2015). *Substance abuse treatment and the stages of change* (2nd ed.). Guilford.

Corey, G. (1995). *Theory and practice of group counseling* (4th ed.). Brooks/Cole.

Corey, G. (2004). *Theory and practice of group counseling: Student manual* (6th ed.). Brooks/Cole.

Corey, G. (2016). *Theory and practice of group counseling* (10th ed.). Cengage.

Corey, G., & Corey, M. S. (1992). *Groups: Process and practice* (4th ed.). Brooks/Cole.

Egolf, D. B. (2001). *Forming, storming, norming, performing.* Writers Club.

French, J., & Raven, B. (1959). The basis of social power. In D. D. Cartwright (Ed.), *Studies on social power* (pp. 150–167). Ann Arbor: University of Michigan, Institute for Social Research.

Generes, W. R. (2024). *Group therapy v. individual therapy: Uses, benefits, & effectiveness.* American Addiction Centers. https://americanaddictioncenters.org/therapy-treatment/group-individual

Greanias, T., & Siegel, S. (2000). Dual diagnosis. In J. R. White & A. S. Freeman (Eds.), *Cognitive-behavioral group therapy for specific problems and populations* (pp. 149–173). American Psychological Association.

Haddock, L. R., & Sheperts, D. S. (2020). Chapter 10: Group counseling for treatment in addictions. In D. Capuzzi & M. D. Stauffer (Eds.), *Foundations of addictions counseling* (4th ed., pp. 208–230). Pearson.

Hersey, P., & Blanchard, K. (1982). *Management of organizational behavior: Utilizing human resources* (4th ed., pp. 176). Prentice-Hall.

Ibrahim, M. (2021, March 30). Tuckman's theory-team development. https:www.linkedin.com/pulse/tuckmans-theory-team-development-mohamed-ibrahim-bpharm-cmas

Ingersoll, K. S., Wagner, C. C., & Gharib, S. (2002). *Motivational groups for community substance abuse programs.* Mid-Atlantic ATTC.

Kinney, J. (2003). *Loosening the grip.* McGraw-Hill.

Malhotra, A., Mars, J. A., & Baker, J. (2024). *Group therapy.* National Institutes of Health (NIH). https://www.ncbi.nlm.nih.gov/books/NBK549812/

Margolis, R. D., & Zweben, J. E. (1998). *Treating patients with alcohol and other drug problems: An integrated approach.* American Psychological Association.

Miller, G. (2021). *Learning the language of addiction counseling* (5th ed.). Wiley.

Miller, G. (2024a, October). *Facilitating SUD recovery: Practical suggestions for medical professionals.* NC Psychiatry and Behavioral Health Series Webinar (online).

Miller, G. (2024b, October). *Substance use disorder (SUD) group counseling & group community building: Motivational interviewing focus-Part 2.* Workshop for Addiction Professionals of North Carolina (online).

Miller, G., Kirkley, D., & Willis, M. (1995, January). *Blending two worlds: Supporting group functions within an addictions' framework.* Paper presented at the meeting of the Third National Conference of the Association for Specialists in Group Work, Athens, GA.

Miller, W. R., Forcehimes, A. A., & Zweben, A. (2019). *Treating addiction: A guide for professionals.* Guilford.

National Institutes of Health (NIH). (2023). *Dual diagnosis.* https://medlineplus.gov/dualdiagnosis.html

Raven, B. H., & Kruglanski, A. W. (1975). Conflict and power. In D. G. Single (Ed.), *The structure of conflict* (pp. 177–219). Academic Press.

SAMHSA. (2005). *Substance abuse treatment: Group therapy.* Treatment Improvement Protocol (TIP 41) Series. https://www.ncbi.nlm.nih.gov/books/NBK64214/#ch2.s14

SAMHSA. (2021). *Group therapy in substance use treatment.* Advisory. https://library.samhsa.gov/sites/default/files/pep20-02-01-020.pdf

Tuckman, B. W. (1965). Developmental sequence in small groups. *Psychological Bulletin, 63* (6), 384–399.

Vannicelli, M. (1995). Group psychotherapy with substance abusers and family members. In A. M. Washton (Ed.), *Psychotherapy and substance abuse* (pp. 337–356). Guilford Press.

Vassar. (2019). *What is a pre-group meeting?* https://offices.vassar.edu/wp-content/uploads/sites/31/2020/03/what-is-a-pre-group-meeting.pdf

Yalom, I. D. (1985). *The theory and practice of group psychotherapy* (3rd ed.). Basic Books.

Yalom, I. D., & Leszcz, M. (2020). *The theory and practice of group psychotherapy* (6th ed.). Basic Books.

Yamashita, A., Yoshioka, S., & Yajima, Y. (2021). *Resilience and related factors as predictors of relapse risk in patients with substance use disorder: A cross-sectional study.* https://link.springer.com/article/10.1186/s13011-021-00377-8

Zell, E., & Stockus, C. A. (2025). Social support and psychological adjustment: A quantitative synthesis of 60 meta-analyses. *American Psychologist, 80* (1), 33–46.

3

Group Exercises

PERSONAL REFLECTIONS

From March 2023 through December 2024, I worked with 14 experienced substance use disorders (SUD) counselors (and 1 group of counselors) as consultants to this book. All of them have SUD group counseling skills I trust and respect. These counselors, who worked in various settings (e.g., inpatient/outpatient) and formats (e.g., in person/online/hybrid) as well as having different and therapeutic goals (e.g., abstinence-based, harm reduction), provided me with feedback on the exercises used in the 1st edition of this book. Some of the consultants tried out new exercises I developed for group work and provided me with feedback while others, in their feedback to me, included exercises they have used in their groups. All of them work with diverse clients and themselves are from diverse populations; thus, their feedback expanded on the diversity concerns they and their SUD clients may experience in the context of group counseling.

Based on their feedback, I have reorganized the exercises to fit the formats counselors need to use. Note that some of the consultants shifted the exercises into categories that fit them and their style. For example, some used exercises listed under Opening exercises for opening exercises and group process exercises or for both opening and closing exercises. The categories of the exercises have been separated, when appropriate, to those that fit an in person-only category; an online-only category; and those that fit into an in person/online category. The 1st edition of this book was designed for in person counseling groups because, in 2012, that was the format of SUD group counseling. At the present time, SUD counselors, in addition to working in various settings with various therapeutic goals, now have SUD groups that occur in various formats (e.g., in person; online; in person/online [hybrid]). Thus, it was necessary to change the organization of the exercise to assist counselors in using them in various formats. Remember that whether in person or online, clients are more likely to recall what they learn if stories/metaphor, humor, experiential activity/play, or music are used to convey information through an exercise.

In terms of exercises used for online groups, some specific comments need to be made. First, many of the activities listed for in person groups can be shifted to online groups; however, both counselor and clients need to be creative and flexible in this application and be aware that online activities require more planning on the front end of group preparation. For example, the "Word Letters Missing" exercise (see "General Opening Group Exercises") can be turned into a "recovery hangman" on a virtual white board function with telehealth groups where the counselor chooses the recovery word, and this is discussed in group. Second, additional examples of online tools are: (1) for exercises that involve lists, the chat option may assist in the use of the exercise, (2) for exercises that involve the use of quotes or readings, a website link may be useful, and (3) for music exercises, the counselor can play the music and copy the lyrics into the telehealth chat. Third, certain exercises (e.g., nonverbals; PVC pipes; family exercises) are simply not easily adaptable to an online format.

In general, counselors conducting groups online are encouraged to find ways to: express their presence; personalize the technology to fit them and their counseling style; remember that no one knows everything there is to know about technology; practice self-care by making oneself comfortable, being calm, and being patient with oneself; develop strategies for working online that focus on client welfare; consult with supervisors/mentors/colleagues regarding online group development and maintenance; stay in touch with one's professional organizations for guidelines in working in this format; and receive training specifically focused on telehealth groups (Miller, 2024). Additionally, in a summary of articles on online group work, Okech (2024) states that counselors using online formats need to learn about how to manage trust and conflict through emotional regulation in online settings through specific interventions in addition to how the format can impact group cohesion and communication. This may be especially important along "fault lines" where there are differences in group members in terms of cultural or social background factors (Penarroja et al., 2024).

Also, Ni et al. (2023) summarizes the contrast of online v. in-person groups as follows: the effectiveness of online groups is the same as in-person groups with therapeutic factors still operating, but both relational issues and a counselor's presence are challenges. These challenges encourage counselors to know their technology tools prior to using them in online groups so the focus can be on interpersonal dynamics.

Finally, some areas, such as family and feelings exploration, may be addressed in other treatment areas for the SUD client.

With all the exercises included in this section, counselors need to sensitively apply them to their population (e.g., regarding touch); be aware that processing exercises requires time; and continually monitor the nonverbals of group members for possible triggering (e.g., substance use; trauma) in response to the exercise. Also, minimal materials are required for these exercises and are generally available to a counselor, whatever counseling format used by the SUD counselor. If some specific, unique materials are mentioned in an exercise (e.g., hula hoops for an in person group), these materials can be substituted with items that are more readily accessible (e.g., chairs for an in person group). In another example, for online groups: (1) some online platforms have a paint/picture/virtual white board option where group members can interact with a virtual white board allowing for group interaction and (2) clients can be asked to bring a pen and paper to their online group.

For some exercises, notations are made, and cautions are noted for SUD counselors following the exercise description as well as suggestions for responding to these cautions or suggestions in general. Counselors need to be sure their clients are not triggered to use substances as a result of group exercises by both listening to their verbal responses as well as their nonverbal responses—clients need to leave group with a sense of safety. For example, some exercises (e.g., SUD Goodbye Letter exercise; Blindfold exercises; Obituary exercises) may arouse intense feelings in the SUD client.

Counselors are encouraged to work flexibly with these exercises to fit the needs and interests of the population (e.g., setting, format, therapeutic goal). As with the example described in the previous paragraph for in person groups, a male therapeutic community population may not be open to using hula hoops, but they may be open to using chairs, and the setting may accommodate chairs more readily. Another example is with language used with the exercises. There are counselors in the SUD field who strongly believe that the phrase "drug of choice" is not appropriate because clients use an "SUD drug of abuse," not one of "choice" or "addiction." Counselors are encouraged to change the language of the exercises to fit their philosophical approach. Also, the organization the counselor works for may require counselors to adapt the exercises in terms of language used. For example, an organization may prohibit the use of spiritual- or religious-related terms such as "Higher Power" or "Serenity Prayer" requiring the counselor to reshape these exercises.

When working with the transgender population within a group, be sensitive to the use of pronouns. "He/she/they" or "They" includes nonbinary people, and this author's choice of term is an attempt to be inclusive. The author encourages counselors to make their own pronoun choice and to keep in mind that we, as counselors, are committed to establishing an equal relationship where clients feel supported in sharing and using their appropriate pronouns if and when they feel ready to do so. Also, counselors are encouraged to avoid dividing a group by gender for an exercise because group members may be uncomfortable identifying themselves as transgender and run the risk of re-experiencing trauma related to their being transgender that led to their SUD. Instead, counselors are encouraged to have them count off or dividing up the group by interests or other factors that are not discriminatory. We make this commitment to an equal relationship no matter how "complicated" it may make us feel in the relationship because of our commitment to the welfare of the client. The goal is to do no harm to a vulnerable population.

Specific time frames are also not provided because SUD groups vary in the length of time given the population, setting, format, and therapeutic goals. Groups may run from 30 to 90 minutes. Exercises may run for a portion of the group time allowed or for the entire length of a group depending on both the leader's and members' interest and involvement with the exercise. Additionally, group counselors need to stress to members that everyone needs to be committed to safety, inclusiveness, and respect so there is a healthy group culture conducive to open communication among group members.

Leaders are encouraged to avoid providing a lot of instructions for the group exercises in order to encourage individual approaches to participation. For example, when asking group members to draw a picture of their SUD (Icebreaker Exercise), the provision of an example may limit the group members' drawings, whereas a general instruction to draw a picture will encourage members to draw on their own worldviews.

Some exercises might be enhanced with demonstration of the exercise before the group becomes involved. For example, in the SUD trial exercise (SUD Recovery Exercise), the leader may want to make a statement proving that SUD is a disease followed by a statement that it is not and then pretend to be the judge and jury responding to those statements.

Note that homework assignments are not stated with the exercise because the counselor may lack the population, setting, format, and therapeutic goals conducive to homework. Many, if not all, exercises may have a homework component included if the leader so chooses.

The techniques of the 1st edition (e.g., Icebreakers, Addiction Recovery, Family/Relationships/Culture, Feelings Exploration, Group Community Building, Self-Esteem, Recovery Skills: Communication/Mindfulness/Problem-Solving, Values, Openers, Closers) have been reorganized into the formats of an in person–only category; an online-only category; and those that fit into an in person/online category. That has required the 1st edition exercises to be shifted to a more appropriate format and, possibly, renamed to better meet the needs of the SUD counselor and SUD client population.

The following are closing comments for this section:

1. Use exercises in various mental health settings (not just SUD) as well as integrated into individual, couple, and therapy settings.
2. Follow a process for exercises involving a term (e.g., "courage"), by asking an open-ended question to the entire group ("What is courage?"), and then following it with a definition ("Courage is the ability to do something you are afraid of.") before processing the term with the group.
3. Remember that group counseling is not individual counseling with one member while other members watch-rather, it is the entire group that is the client.

4. Create a safe, respectful environment, a healthy community by setting expectations of group member behaviors that create such a culture in the group thereby encouraging vulnerability. Note that this process begins by the counselor asking the self-reflective questions: "How can I be helpful in this group?" "What can I do to be helpful?"

5. Provide realistic hope for members to change.

6. Switch the SUD to another disease, such as diabetes or cancer, when confused about how to address the SUD.

7. Be aware that SUD clients live in a culture that encourages addictive tendencies.

8. Know what resources are available and consult with other professionals as needed.

9. Use Motivational Interviewing theory and techniques to assist members in exploring their SUD and being exposed to a menu of options they can choose from as they follow their own path in their SUD recovery as well as the Stages of Change Model to understand where they are on their journey.

10. Hold them accountable for their behavior by focusing on their behavior, but not judging them.

ICEBREAKERS

These are exercises that help the group get to know each other or bond with each other.

In Person Only (Versions)

Introductions (In Person)

○ <u>Introductions (through accomplishments)</u>: Give the group members index cards and have them write down one or two things that they are proud of accomplishing in their lives. Have them exchange the cards and then introduce the person whose card they have. The person being introduced must stand up, and everybody should give them a cheer for whatever accomplishment that they've had.

○ <u>Introductions (through other clients)</u>: Pair clients and have them get to know each other for about 5 or 10 minutes. Then bring them back into the big group and have them introduce each other to the group. <u>Caution</u>: This exercise can take a lot of time. <u>Suggestion</u>: When pairing clients, try to be sensitive to the safety of trans and nonbinary group members by choosing partners for them that have not expressed any transphobic or homophobic sentiments during introductions or screening.

O <u>Introductions (through other clients—drug specific)</u>: Have clients introduce themselves to each other, talk about their drug of choice, and their expectations for treatment. Then bring them back into the big group and have them introduce each other to the group.

O <u>Introductions (through food)</u>: Have everybody say their first names and then add to that a food of some kind, such as "My name is Pat and I like pie."

O <u>Introductions (through hopes/dreams)</u>: Have each client share one hope/dream with the group. You may hear something like: "I hope I have a family one day." or "I hope that I stay clean." or "I hope that I'm stable someday."

O <u>Introductions (through leader)</u>: Have a worksheet called "getting to know me" and have people fill it out and pass the finished sheets to the leader. Then, read them out loud without telling people whose profile is being read. <u>Caution</u>: The leader needs the information before the exercise is used in the group. <u>Suggestion</u>: For gender, have a write-in option as well as a write-in option for pronouns. For pronouns, a simple check-box could ask: "Are you comfortable using these pronouns in the group? If not, what pronouns would you like me to use when referring to you in the group?"

O <u>Introductions (through location)</u>: Identify where individuals live in the state and have them talk a little bit about where they live and that type of thing. <u>Caution</u>: This exercise may take a lot of time and, for some clients, trigger an urge to use.

O <u>Introductions (through their names)</u>: Have group members write down their names along with an adjective that can describe them and that starts with the first letter of their last name. This helps the leader to gauge some of the clients' self-perspective—how they feel about themselves. Then have an open discussion about what each person wrote. <u>Caution</u>: This exercise could be paired with the exercise above: Introductions (through food). <u>Suggestion</u>: Include pronouns as a part of this exercise modeling your own pronouns first when introducing yourself.

○ <u>Introductions (through partner)</u>: Separate the group members into pairs and have them introduce themselves to each other. Then bring them back together as a class and have each one introduce his/her partner to the group. <u>Caution</u>: This exercise takes a lot of time. <u>Suggestion</u>: When pairing clients, try to be sensitive to the safety of trans and non-binary group members by choosing partners for them that have not expressed any transphobic or homophobic sentiments during introductions or screening.

○ <u>Introductions (through self-facts)</u>: In the beginning of a group, have group members move into smaller groups based on what they have in common. For example: Who was born in North Carolina? Who has a pet? Who is left-handed? Who plays a musical instrument or sings? Who has blue/brown eyes? Who has been to a foreign country? <u>Caution</u>: This exercise takes a lot of time.

○ <u>Introduction (through topic)</u>: The counselor identifies a recovery-related topic, which might be about relapse, parents, feelings (shame, guilt), etc. Whoever in the group relates to that topic starts a discussion about it.

○ <u>Introductions (through trivia)</u>: Give everyone a sheet of paper with five or six questions on it and then ask them to go around and find out who can answer those questions. For instance, if somebody was born in Boston, Massachusetts, then you have to go around the room and ask people if they were born in Boston or not. It's a way of getting people to know a little bit about each other. <u>Caution</u>: Make sure, in the choosing of trivia, that the trivia avoids negatively impacting client self-esteem and/or their view (as well as others' views) of their intelligence. Also, this exercise takes a lot of time.

<u>Suggestion</u>: Focus on it being a fun activity where clients learn fun things about each other and build in adequate time for the exercise.

○ <u>Name Introduction</u>: Have the leader introduce themselves by name, for example, "My name is Andre." Then the person next to them must introduce themselves as well as the person who just went, such as, "My name is Kate, and that was Andre." The third person will introduce themselves as well as the two previous people and so on until everyone has had a turn. <u>Suggestion</u>: Include pronouns as a part of this exercise modeling your own pronouns first when introducing yourself.

Online Adaptations of Icebreaker Introductions

Each member uses the chat function to direct message to the group leader prior to the start of the activity. Here, they submit the introduction exercise information, and the group leader makes each statement and the group collectively chooses who that information belongs to in the group.

Additional Exercises (In Person)

○ <u>SUD Picture</u>: Have the members draw a picture of their SUD and discuss the pictures in group. <u>Suggestion</u>: If using this exercise with an online platform, follow the suggestions made above in the "Personal Reflections" section.

○ <u>Favorite Meal</u>: Have each participant describe the appetizer, the main course, and the drink they would have with their favorite meal. This exercise may bring up warm memories that the clients have of spending time with family and friends. The exercise gets everybody talking together about things that they like for meals, discover commonalities among themselves, and invite exploration of why meals are important to them. <u>Caution</u>: This exercise can make people hungry; trigger negative memories of mealtimes; and be frustrating for clients in settings where they have no meal choice (e.g., inpatient settings). <u>Suggestion</u>: If using this exercise with an online platform, follow the suggestions made above in the "Personal Reflections" section.

GENERAL OPENING GROUP EXERCISES

O   <u>Four-Legged Stool</u>: Use this visual diagram (Figure 3.1) as a check-in for how group members are doing as each member runs through the different legs of the stool. It teaches them about the importance of balance in their recovery as it relates to self-care. <u>Suggestions</u>:

1.   Make sure to talk with them about "pretty good" self-care so they are not trying to do it perfectly but instead are trying to make progress in each area doing the best they can do for that day. One way of doing this is through encouraging them to practice checking in with themselves frequently as to if they feel **H**ungry, **A**ngry, **L**onely, **T**ired (**HALT**) and respond to those needs ASAP;

2.   Be aware that group members may want to expand the 4th leg and include aspects such as social (e.g., being more social with others) and that they may raise concerns about only having balance in a few of the legs thereby throwing the stool off balance. This can lead

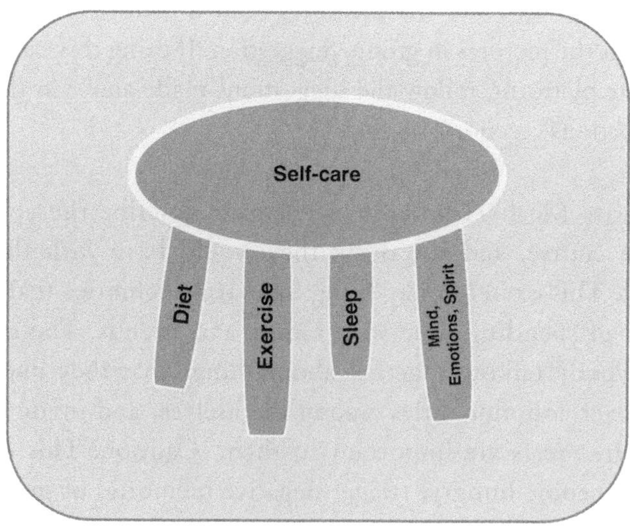

Figure 3.1   Self-care. *Source*: Miller (2024). Academic violence and bullying of faculty. Cognella Inc.

to discussions of a more balanced recovery by expanding their social life and responding to self-care barriers that present themselves; and

3. Ask them the following questions: (a) *"What routines/rituals are helpful to you?"*; (b) *"What is the best way to start your day?"*; (c) *"How might you regain your balance in a day if you lose it?"*; and (d) *"When you are afraid, ask yourself these safety questions: 'Who feels safe to me right now?' 'Where is a safe place for me right now?'"*.

○ <u>Kindness</u>: Ask each member to describe an act of kindness they observed that day—without giving away any names of the people they saw do them. Another option is to have them report an act of kindness they did since the last group and think about this/journal about it through the week.

○ <u>Meditation Word/Meaning</u>: Read a meditation section out of a book and then have each member of the group choose a word of the day or a meaning that they got out of the meditation and write that down or simply think about it. Follow this with five minutes of complete silence and then open up the group and have each member tell the word they gave and what it means to them, how it affects them or what part it plays in their lives today. Then have group members respond to each person's reaction to the word and/or meaning.

○ <u>Myth or Truth?</u>: Have group members select a topic such as relationships, communications, anger, substance abuse, feelings, etc. Then have each member say "myth or truth" and make a statement about the topic. Allow them to express what they think of or know about that topic. Write everything down in a format they can all read, and sort out with them, through group processing, what is true for this topic and what is not true for this topic.

○ <u>Positive Statements</u>: Have each client go around and tell other group members something positive about them. It needs to be anything positive, such as "You have a nice shirt on," or "I like the way you've done your hair." <u>Caution</u>: This exercise can result in members judging each other and focusing on physical appearance. <u>Suggestion</u>: Encourage members to avoid judging others by holding them accountable for feedback they give to others and by commenting on aspects other than physical appearance.

○ <u>Question List</u>: Have a number of questions written down and give the list to each person. Have each member go through the questions and pick which ones they want to answer. The questions can include things like, "What was the dinner like with your family? How are you feeling?"

○ <u>The Story of My Name</u>: Ask each group member to respond individually by completing the following statements (making sure to tell them it is okay if they don't know the answer): "My full name is ____." "I was named by ____." "My first and middle names were named after ____." "The name I like to be called is ____." "The reason(s) I like people to call me by that name is ____." "My name is unique in this way ____." <u>Caution</u>: Be aware there may be painful memories that arise in response to this exercise that tends to draw out life stories.

○ <u>Truth or Lie?</u>: Have group members (and the leader) tell two things that are true about themselves and then a lie. The answers are put on a format they can all read, and the other group members have to guess what is true and what is not true about the member.

○ <u>"What If?"</u>: Get everyone to write a silly "what-if" question. It can be any type of question such as "What if Albert Einstein was my father?" Ask for a volunteer to read the question out loud and give a silly answer such as "Then I wouldn't know how to tie my shoes." Repeat the process for every "what if" question statement. For example, in answer to the question, "What if Christmas was in July?" and their answer could be, "We'd ride surfboards instead of sleds." This can be a fun, light-hearted exercise.

○ <u>Word Letters Missing</u>: Write a word with letters missing in a format everyone can read and have the group try to guess what the word is. Try to relate that word to whatever topic the group will be working on that day.

In Person Only (Versions)

Verbal Exercise

○ <u>Personal Experience Disclosure</u>: Have one less hula hoop than the number of people in the group: If there are ten individuals, have nine hula hoops. Nine people take a hula hoop and stand in a circle. The person without the hula hoop stands in the middle and makes a statement about something they have done or something that has happened to them. If one of the people in the circle has experienced the same thing, they have to exchange places with the person in the middle (only one person makes the exchange). This can continue until all group members have been in the middle.

Nonverbal Exercises

◆ Have the group break into pairs, and have one person mirror the other's movement one-on-one with no touching.

◆ Have one person in the group do a pantomime. Another person should walk up to them and ask them what they are doing. The person doing the pantomime answers with something irrelevant to the pantomime. For example, they may be acting like they are driving a car, but when asked what they are doing, they might say, "Picking my nose." Then the person watching needs to create a pantomime based on that verbal response—they need to pick their nose. Continue this until everyone in the group has participated.

◆ Have one person lead the group in a nonverbal movement, with the others following. Then the group leader should name someone else in the group and have them lead the group in a nonverbal movement. Continue until everyone in the group has participated.

◆ Have the group get into pairs, and have one person give the other person a shoulder rub, switching after one to two minutes. The exercise should be done in silence, with the understanding that no one is required to participate, and they can choose to stop the exercise at any point.

◆ Divide the group in half, and have one half of the group sit in a circle and act as the receiver. The other half of the group is on the outside as the giver. A person in the giver group touches the shoulder of a person in the receiver group for about 30 seconds. Then, the person being touched leaves the chair and the other person sits down.

SUD RECOVERY

These are exercises that facilitate awareness of SUD recovery.

In Person Only

○ <u>Balloons</u>: Take into group five or six balloons of different colors. Ask one client what the most important thing is in his/her life and have the client take a balloon and toss that balloon from hand to hand. While doing this, distract the client from the balloon and challenge them by asking "Can you keep the balloon up with one foot in the air?" Then, start throwing other balloons into the mix and have the client try to juggle those with the original balloon. The new balloons stand for other people or life areas that are important to the client. Use this as a starting point to talk in the group about stress management in recovery and how to keep the most important things in our lives up in the air.

○ <u>Blindfold Experience 1</u>: Pair clients up and have one of the clients blindfolded and the other acting as a seeing-eye dog. Have them tour the facility blindfolded: up the elevator, down the stairs, through the kitchen, bathroom, etc., along the way letting them touch, feel, and smell things. Using it as a life metaphor, after the experience, process in group how life is pretty much a blind journey that we stumble our way through, so we need to learn to trust someone under those circumstances. Generally, the clients feel helpless, confused, and lost during this exercise, and this is pretty much the state in which they come in for treatment. By having someone else help guide them through, hopefully it will establish some trust that they can depend on someone else other than themselves to help them find their way through life.

○ <u>Blindfold Experience 2</u>: Blindfold one group member and take them out of the group. Give each group member a piece of paper, and have them write down one obstacle in life. Then choose two people and take them away from the group. Explain to those two people that one of them will be a support system for the blindfolded person, and the other will be a barrier for the person. Then have the group members put their obstacles on the floor. Explain to the two people that they can hold onto the blindfolded person's arms, but they can't jerk them, they can only guide them in a direction. During this exercise, those two people will have to get the blindfolded person through these obstacles. What you want them to see is that this support person, or sponsor, is going to try to guide them through the right path—guide them so as to not step on these obstacles. The barrier person, who is going to be louder than the sponsor, is going to be pulling the person toward the obstacles and saying things like "Come this way, I won't steer you wrong, come this way, come on! Come on!" At the same time, the support person is saying, "No! Remember what happened to you last time? This is not a good road! Come this way!" They can use whatever words they want to persuade the blindfolded person. If the blindfolded person steps on an obstacle, they have relapsed, and they have to start over again. Do that a couple of times. Group members see a lot of struggles. When the group member makes it past the obstacles, stop the exercise and have everyone sit down and process what happened. Ask the person who was blindfolded, "What made you choose to decide who you trusted?" or, "How did you feel blindfolded?" It leads to a lot of conversation about how they made up their mind about who to listen to. At the end of the group, talk about what a good support system is, how you decide who you will trust, and how to make good choices.

○ <u>Box of Stuff</u>: Start off with a box of random, nondangerous household items. Have group members pick one item from the box of stuff that they will use to describe who they are, where they are in their treatment, what they are there to work on, and what they want to work on in the future. <u>Note</u>: This could also be used with crystals/stones where the member could use the texture and color to describe themselves as a person.

○ <u>Carnival Ride</u>: Have group members find a place in the room to stand and ask them to mimic a carnival or amusement park ride that represents their past experiences with their SUD. Once they begin to do this, go around and ask them to describe what the ride is, how it relates to their historical experiences, and the feelings they have about that experience.

○ <u>Higher Power Jar</u>: Use different kinds of jars so the participants can pick whichever jar they want, and hand out little strips of paper in all different colors. Instruct group members, "Whatever you want to give to your Higher Power, write it on the piece of paper and put it into the jar." Once a week, for each client, dump all of the papers out of their jar and read each one. If they are still holding onto what a particular paper says, put it back into the jar. If they are no longer worried about it or not holding onto it, throw it away.

○   <u>Hot Seat</u>: Have the group form a circle and put a swivel chair in the center. A group member sits in the chair and tells the story of their use history. After the client tells their story, have members ask a question of the client, and the leader throws a piece of candy to the member who asks the question.

○   <u>Leader as SUD</u>: In this exercise, the leader plays the role of an SUD. Group members write down 10 of their most valued people, places, or things in order of which is most important to them. Then the leader, as the SUD, goes around and takes away all of the valuable things (e.g., rip up what they wrote, step on what they wrote). Then, group members process how their SUD does the same thing to them and discuss what kinds of things they need to do to prevent that.

○   <u>Marble Transfer in PVC Pipes</u>: Put different sizes of PVC pipe into a bucket. Have each group member come up and get a piece of pipe and stand in a line leading up to the bucket. Give a marble to the person at the beginning of the line, farthest away from the bucket. The group has to work together, rolling the marble through the PVC pipes, to get the marble into the bucket. Eventually, the marble drops and they have to start all over again. This exercise can be used to start a discussion about relapse, how it is not the end of the world, and about how they can develop tools to rely on other people and ask for help.

○   <u>Me Bags</u>: Give the group members paper grocery bags and scissors and have them cut out and paste things from magazines on the outside of the bags that they want people to see. Then have them cut out things they don't want people to see and place them on the inside of the bags. Then have them process through that exercise by pulling out items and explaining to the group what those are and how these hidden aspects of themselves impact their recovery.

○ <u>Motivational Change Quotes</u>: Out of a jar that contains motivational change quotes, have a group member choose a motivational quote about change out of the jar and read it. Then have the group members discuss what that quote means to them, what they think that quote represents in terms of their recovery, and how it's significant to them and their recovery. Keep drawing quotes as needed to facilitate the discussion of change in their recovery.

○ <u>Pass-the-Basket</u>: Put a number of recovery-related discussion topics (e.g., staying sober; forgiveness; trauma; family) on slips of paper and place them into a basket. Everybody gets to choose a slip of paper and talk about whatever the topic is.

○ <u>Pillow as SUD</u>: Bring in a bunch of pillows, have everybody in the group pick one, and write on a board a description of the pillows: Are they soft? What do they symbolize? Why do we have them? How many do we have? Then ask the clients, "How many of these relate to when you were actively using? Was the drug something to comfort you that signified feeling relaxed, feeling peaceful?" Then each group member is told that that pillow now symbolizes their SUD for the day, and just like the SUD, they can't put it down and they can't hide it. They may try to mask it underneath things, but everybody knows it's there. Clients have to imagine they are holding onto that pillow all day long; they can't put it down—even when using the bathroom. Then at the end of group, after holding onto the pillow for the entire group, they are told they can now release the pillow (their SUD), let it go, because it no longer has to be something they have to constantly carry around with them and bind themselves to. They can keep the pillow as a symbol to remind them that they do carry these things around but they can put them down. <u>Note</u>: This could be changed to a small teddy bear or crystal.

○ <u>Posttreatment Goals</u>: Have a group member identify a goal they would like to achieve when they get out of treatment. Have another member write the goal down on a piece of paper and stand at the opposite end of the room. Then, have the group member identify three obstacles that can keep them from reaching their goal, and have other members write these obstacles on pieces of paper and hold them up. Assign roles to the remaining group members, such as AA, therapy, couple's counseling, parenting classes, etc. Ask the original client to try to move toward their goal and have the group members who are holding the obstacles try to prevent him/her from moving toward their goal. The client must stop at each obstacle and consider how it would be best to handle that obstacle. They may also reach out to the other group members who are playing the roles such as AA. Continue until they have dealt with each one of the obstacles. This can help the client have a better understanding of how and who to ask for help when obstacles arise. Have a group discussion afterward and let other members discuss things they have identified with.

○   Recovery Questions: Write down enough recovery-related questions for each group member, such as: "What is your biggest fear about staying sober?" and "Where do you see yourself in five years?" Have a group member pick a question from the pile and answer that question. After he/she answers that question, have the next person pick a question and answer it until all group members have had a chance to respond.

○   Recovery Wall: Have the group members stand up and position themselves in relation to the wall in such a way that it signifies the degree of safety they feel about not relapsing: the closer they stand to the wall, the more danger they are in; the farther away from the wall, the safer they are. Have them talk about what that distance behind them means and what techniques they are using to give them confidence about that distance they are standing from the wall.

○   Rocks in the Backpack: Take rocks and write negative emotions on them, such as fear, hate, resentment, etc. Have the group members put the rocks into a backpack and have each carry the backpack around with him/her. After the group members have taken off and put down the backpack, ask them what it was like to let go of the backpack. This exercise demonstrates how they carry around feelings and don't let them go; it can lead into a discussion about the process of letting go.

○ <u>Rubber Ball</u>: Hand a rubber band ball to a client and tell them to ask anyone in the group a treatment-related question. The client asks the question and then throws the ball to the person who they want to answer. After that person answers, that same person asks a question and throws the ball to another client.

○ <u>"Spies"</u>: During the last weekly group and just before group is over, give everyone a piece of paper that has "S-P-I-E-S" written down the side. This stands for Spiritual, Physical, Intellectual, Emotional, and Social. Each client has to fill in on the paper what they are going to do over the weekend (or the break) in order to be healthy in each particular area. For example, for "spiritual," they could say, "I'm going to attend a church service" or "I'm going to go for a sunrise walk on the beach." For "physical," they could say, "I'm going to work out; I'm going to do 20 sit-ups." Try to get them to be as specific as possible about what they're going to do. It's a way for them to think about the group even though they're not there and about what their goals are. During the following group, review each one's paper and what they did over the weekend.

○ <u>SUD Empty Chair</u>: Take two empty chairs and put them in the middle of the room. One chair represents the SUD, and the other chair represents the client. The client sits in the SUD chair first and tries to entice the client chair to use again by telling the chair the benefits of using. Then have the client move and sit in the client chair and talk back to the disorder. Have them discuss the consequences of using again and why they don't want to go back there. The exercise works well in breaking through the client's denial.

○ <u>SUD Graveyard Visit</u>: Have everyone write a letter of goodbye to their SUD, and then take them to a graveyard and have the group members stand among the gravestones and read their letters.

○ <u>SUD Talking</u>: Have a client sit in a chair by themselves and have other clients play the SUD. The clients playing the SUD should walk toward the client in the chair and entice them to use by telling them all the wonderful things about using and how fun it's going to be and so forth. As they get closer and closer to the client with more and more persuasive arguments, the client admits that they are crumbling. Then take another person from the group, who may represent the client's significant other, and that person stands next to the client, touches the client, and starts talking back to the SUD. The disorder starts talking again from the back of the room while walking toward the client persuasively giving the argument to use substances. As the client's significant other argues against the disorder, keep adding support people (e.g., friends, group members, 12-step groups, sponsors), and as these people are added around the client sitting in the chair, the disorder can't be heard over the din of the support people talking against the disorder and the disorder can't find a way through the circle support which completes surrounds the client (the disorder can't get close to the recovering SUD client). It really helps demonstrate how the client can't go it alone and the benefits of using other people in their life to help them stay clean.

○ <u>Trashcan Activity</u>: Sit in a circle and put a trashcan in the middle. Give the clients five pieces of paper stapled together and have them write down on each sheet of paper something important they will lose if they continue to use. On the first sheet of paper, it may say something like "clothing" and the second one something like "food." Then they might have "house," "children," and eventually they get to "life"—the last one. Then, on the board write the statement, "If I continue to use *blank* and do not stop, I will lose *blank*." Go around the circle and have everyone repeat that statement and fill it in with whatever substance they were using as well as whatever they will lose. Then have them rip off their first sheet of paper and throw it in the trashcan. Go around the circle again, repeating the exercise until they have thrown all of their pages away. It's interesting to see how the mood changes as the exercise progresses. At first it can be somewhat humorous, but when they start to throw significant others (be sure to have clients use their names), and eventually their lives are thrown away, the atmosphere changes. It is helpful to process what it would feel like to throw all those things away and to be able to say, "If I continue to do this, then this will be what happens."

○ <u>Using Names</u>: Have group members write a street name that they used when they were using on a piece of paper and then take that paper and burn it on an outside grill with the group standing around in a circle.

The client has the opportunity to tell that name goodbye. <u>Caution</u>: For trans or nonbinary people in the group, be aware that this can stir challenging feelings for them.

○ <u>"Win, Lose, or Draw"</u>: Have a group member draw something on the board and have everybody guess the title of the picture, with the rule that the person doing the drawing can't talk. If someone says "bird," and "bird" is a part of the title, the person doing the drawing has to write it on the board. There can be different categories, such as movies, books, TV, as in charades. The exercise is useful for demonstrating that one can have fun when one is not high.

In Person/Online

○ <u>Board of Directors</u>: Start out by explaining what a board of directors is in case someone doesn't know (a group of people who have authority to make decisions about an organization). Then ask the clients to draw a rectangle and put three people on either side and two people at the head. Ask them to identify who is in what role: director, president, support people, etc. Through the process of talking about the people they chose and what their roles are, it might become clear to them that they might have to ask some of their "board members" to leave. Ask the clients, "Does someone need to ask somebody to leave the board? Are they supportive of your recovery?" This helps them to start thinking in terms of who they're going to ask for advice and who they might have to kick off the board and who to put on the board so they're more supportive of their recovery.

○ <u>Client Story Disclosure</u>: Ask new clients to share their SUD history—from the first time they used up to how they have ended up in the group.

○ <u>Dr. Frankenstein's Monster (a.k.a. Fear Monster)</u>: Create a monster—a SUD drug monster based on the negative characteristics or attributes of an SUD person, such as a thief, a liar, poor hygiene, etc., as stated by group members. Then solicit from the group positive attributes of a healthy, sober person: employed, honest, healthy, exerciser, etc. Discuss how they see themselves in their recovery based on these contrasting attributes.

○ <u>Forgiveness #1: Self-forgiveness</u>: Ask clients to list one to five behaviors that they need to forgive themselves for and write a brief summary of each event where they acted out this specific behavior. Process their thoughts/feelings/reactions to this experience. In a future group, this exercise can be built on by having members write a letter to themselves (either during group or outside of the group) that takes responsibility for the behavior while outlining the emotional pain and the how they have continued to punish themselves for their behavior. This letter can be read and processed in the group for each member focusing on how they can practice self-forgiveness now (e.g., rip up/burn the letter).

○ <u>Forgiveness #2: Other—forgiveness</u>: Have clients draw 1 column for the person or organization they have a resentment/anger toward and 1 column for the detailed impact that harm had on them. While the complete exercise does not need to be reviewed for each group member, process each client's thoughts/feelings/reactions to this experience in the group. In a future group, this exercise can be built on by shifting the focus to others they want to seek forgiveness from who are either living or deceased. In this exercise, clients can write a letter to one person they choose that states the wrong they did and expresses remorse for the harm they caused them. This letter can be read and processed in the group for each member focusing on how they can practice self-forgiveness now (e.g., rip up/burn the letter).

○ <u>Growing a New Life</u>: Give group members two illustrations of a tree—the tree should have a trunk, branches, and leaves. One illustration represents the life of their SUD, and the other one represents the new life that they are aspiring to. In the illustration of the life of the SUD, the branches are characteristics or character defects, and the leaves are the consequences or the results of these qualities and behavior. In the illustration of the new life, the branches are qualities the clients are trying to move toward, and the leaves are the fruits of these new qualities.

○ <u>Humor/Laughter in Recovery</u>: Ask these questions to facilitate a discussion of humor/laughter in recovery: (1) *"When is the last time I laughed (a hearty laugh) sober?"*; (2) *"Who (people) makes me laugh in my recovery?"*; (3) *"What makes me laugh?"* (e.g., places, activities); (4) *"What are the barriers to me having a sense of humor? laughing?"* (e.g., stressors in recovery); (5) *"What messages have I received in my life about humor? laughter?"*; (6) *"Where (and with whom) is it safe to share my sense of humor? laugh?"*; and (7) *"How can learning to laugh at little things/laugh at myself help me in my recovery?"*. <u>Caution</u>: Be aware that some clients may have negative associations with laughter especially with being laughed at by others. <u>Suggestion</u>: Be prepared to use prompting questions for question 5 about messages received because clients may default to an answer that humor/laughter is simply necessary and good for their well-being.

○ <u>Issue Exploration</u>: Ask clients to respond to the questions: "What are you working on now in your recovery? What do you feel like you need to work on?" on a sheet of paper. Have clients read their sheets aloud and allow discussion.

○ <u>Journals</u>: Ask the clients where they would like to be in their recovery within the next year, and have them keep journals about that. At the end of each group, offer clients the opportunity to discuss what they wrote about (if they are willing to disclose that information).

○ <u>Life Story Timeline</u>: Have each group member write their life story using a timeline, beginning with the year that they were born up until the present year, sharing and listing significant events that happened in their life. Give them specific examples to write down, like the first time they used substances, the first time they were arrested, the first time they dropped out of school, divorced, moved, and had a death in the family—things that they can remember that stand out in their life. Have them write it down in their free time and bring it back to the group or sketch a timeline out in group. Also have them add to the timeline what they would like to do from this point on.

○ <u>Music—Client Favorite Song</u>: Have group members bring in a song that they feel is representative of them or of some aspect of their life—something that speaks to them. Ask them to write out the words and bring them to the group so everyone in the group can read them. Ask them how they relate to different aspects of the song in terms of their active SUD or recovery from their SUD. Process all group members reactions to the music.

○ <u>Music—Counselor Assignments</u>: Give group members assignments to listen to music that invites them to: (1) Feel more connected to themselves ("I feel okay."); (2) Motivate themselves to stay sober ("I can do this."); and (3) Help themselves relax and be less anxious ("I am safe in the world."). Process reactions in the next group.

○ <u>Music-Counselor Song Choice</u>: Play a song(s) that is important to recovery and ask members how they relate to that song and how it speaks to them.

○ <u>Music-Relaxation Exercise</u>: Play a mellow type of listening music. Have participants close their eyes and do about five minutes of relaxation techniques with them. Then tell them to imagine that they can go wherever they want with whomever they want. Use visualization of a pristine lake or a natural area (somewhere quiet and serene, a good place for them) and some sober activities they might do in that area. After that, come back together, and give them a chance to explain where that took them. This gives a lot of information about what things are comfortable for them and activities they like in their recovery.

○ <u>Music-SUD Comparative Listening Experiences (Active SUD use vs SUD Recovery)</u>: Facilitate a discussion where each group member compares the music they listened to while using alcohol/drugs to the music they listen to now that encourages them in their recovery. Use the following questions to stimulate the discussion: (1) *"What music did you listen to when using alcohol/drugs?", "How did that music impact you?"* and (2) *"What music are you listening to now?", "How does that music impact you in your recovery?"*

○ <u>Music-SUD Triggers</u>: Facilitate a discussion of SUD triggering music (in whatever electronic form they use to listen to music) by asking the following questions: (1) *"What, if any, music triggers trauma for you?"*; (2) *"What, if any, music triggers alcohol/drug use for you?"*; and (3) *"What, if any, music increases your cravings for alcohol/drugs?"* <u>Suggestions</u>: (1) Remember that music triggers are unique to each client and need to be processed as such; and (2) When members struggle with identifying triggering music, consider shifting it to *sounds* that trigger them (e.g., popping sounds for gunshot-related trauma; pill bottles being opened for SUD use and cravings) or give them examples of music that is connected to *partying*.

○ <u>Obituary—Drug of Choice</u>: Have group members write an obituary for their SUD drug of choice.

○ <u>Obituary—Using Versus Sober Obituaries</u>: Get the group members to write out what their obituary might have been if they had died during their using days. Then have them write out an obituary from the point of view of where they hope to be after they have been in recovery for a period of time. Process the contrast between them in the group.

○ <u>Obituary—Write-Up</u>: Ask the clients to write their own obituaries. If they refuse (and often people do), say "If you continue your SUD, then you *are* writing your obituary, and the truth of who you really are is not going to be told." Sometimes they think about it and say "If I continue in this active SUD, I am going to die. Spiritually, once I resume my use, I am dead already because I have taken my higher power out of everything that I've done in my life simply by using." This exercise creates the opportunity for them to see their use in a different light.

○ <u>Play in Recovery</u>: Ask the following questions to facilitate a discussion of the importance of play in recovery: (1) *"What is fun for me?"* (e.g., people, places, activities); (2) *"What are the barriers to me having fun?"* (e.g., time, energy, money); (3). *"What messages have I received in my life about having fun?"*; (4). *"When is the last time I played?"*; (5) *"Who are people in my life who encourage me to play?"*; (6) *"Where (and with whom) is it safe to play?"*; and (7) *"How has my alcohol/drug use influenced my view of play and having fun?"* <u>Cautions</u>: (1) This may be a challenging area for some populations such as those clients who "lived in the streets" from a young age because they may view fun as a weakness; however, it may assist them (and clients in general) in identifying self-limiting beliefs; (2) It is difficult to find a balance between work and play; and (3) This topic may stir painful, unresolved emotions. <u>Suggestions</u>:

1. Since these questions are similar to those in the humor/laughter in recovery exercise in this section, consider combining these two exercises into one exercise that brings together humor, laughter, and play in recovery;

2. Be prepared to use prompting questions for question because clients may tend to default to the answer that play is simply necessary and good for their well-being; and

3. Use this as an icebreaker exercise also.

O <u>Prisoner of SUD</u>: Show a picture of a person in jail with a caption that reads, "Why is this person in jail?" Then tape a caption over it that says, "What is it that keeps you in your own prison of the SUD?" Have each group member process their reactions to this question.

O <u>Protective Wall Drawing</u>: Have everyone draw the walls that they put up to protect themselves from the outside world (money, sleeping, alcohol, drugs, etc.). Then have them explain what is on their piece of paper that they use for walls to protect them from the world.

O <u>Psychological Gardening Drawing</u>: Have members draw a circle in the middle of a piece of paper and put their name in the circle. Around the circle they draw five flower petals. In each petal, they write one word across the bottom for the ground and then they draw a stem from the flower to the ground. Next, they draw four flowers. On the four flowers, they put the names of the people, places, things, or ideas that are supportive to them. Below the ground they draw 10 roots, which are straight lines down. On the roots, they write activities that they do or would like to do. Next, they draw two butterflies, which represent decisions that they made in the past that they are proud of. Finally, they draw four weeds that represent what will get in their way of doing the things that they like to do—this is also known in SUD recovery as "people, places, things" (the terminology may vary) that need to be changed.

○ <u>Recovery Scaling Technique</u>: Use scaling technique questions: "Is anyone here today doing any better in their recovery than they were yesterday/last week?" Rate that improvement on a scale from 1 to 10 (1 is the least you have improved in your recovery and 10 is the most). Comment on *how* you were able to make these improvements." <u>Caution</u>: Watch for a tendency of members to rate themselves high especially when group cohesion is low and they may be concerned about how they appear to others rather than risk being vulnerable. <u>Note</u>: When group cohesion is high, members may tend to be more honest about how they rate self regardless about how other members rate themselves.

○ <u>Recovery Words</u>: Have group members write a word related to recovery. Collect the words and have members choose a word from the list presented to them and then describe the word and what that word means to them. Another variation is to pick a word about recovery and discuss how they can work that into their recovery and make it a part of their lives.

○ <u>Self-Care</u>: Ask the individual clients to do something good for themselves in their recovery and come back and discuss this experience in group. <u>Note</u>: This reminds members that SUD recovery is hard and celebrating their self-care, as well as their accomplishments in this area, is important.

○ <u>Serenity Prayer Analysis</u>: Use this exercise when everybody is feeling overwhelmed and having trouble focusing on what they need to do in treatment. Draw a circle on the board and talk about the Serenity Prayer. Break it up and talk about the word "serenity" and "God grant me serenity to accept the things I cannot change." The outside of the circle stands for the "things I cannot change" and write all those things on the outside of the circle (e.g., someone's spouse's attitude about their SUD, whether or not the courts are going to take away their license, the past, etc.). Then talk about the fact that when saying the Serenity Prayer, they are asking for a Higher Power to give them peace over those things. The center of the circle stands for "courage to change the things I can." Here they can write down the things they can change (e.g., "I can share in group, I can go to a meeting, I can come and sponsor, I can pray, I can do my assigned work"). This brings the focus back to their actions. When people get overwhelmed, there tends to be a focus on the outside of the circle, which are the things they can't change. If they can do three things inside the circle, it will help them become more grounded and be in the here and now.

O   <u>Sober Fun</u>: Discuss how to play and what the clients are going to do with the vacuum in their lives that drugs used to fill. Ask them to think way back into their childhoods about what activities they enjoyed—maybe about what they did with a significant other that was really fun for them. If they answer with something like they went fishing with them, suggest that maybe they take young people fishing. Also ask them to think of something that they had always really wanted to that they have never done. Then explore resources in their community where they could do this sort of thing. Finally, ask them what they are currently doing for fun in their recovery.

O   <u>Stages of Change</u>: Ask each group member what stage of change they are in (precontemplation, contemplation, preparation, action, maintenance, termination), have the person describe how they reached the decision that they were in that stage, and then ask the other members if they agree that the member is in that stage. Follow this process until every group member has an opportunity to share their perception of their stage of change and to receive feedback from other members. <u>Note</u>: This exercise can be used at intervals throughout a group allowing members to note their progression through the stages. Also, it can help members understand group dynamics because of the various stages different group members are in.

O   <u>SUD Goodbye Letter</u>: Have the group members write a letter to their drug(s) of choice. It can start off like they are writing a letter to a friend. Some might write three pages, some just a paragraph. Have them tell the drug everything they liked about it and what the drug took away from them and how it hurt them. Have each member read their letter out loud and then tear their letters up and throw them away. This exercise brings up different emotions, and it also provides a symbolic way of saying goodbye to the drug. <u>Note</u>: This letter writing can be done during the group, given as a homework assignment, or used in the last group for a member who is leaving the group.

o   <u>SUD Trial</u>: Create two opposing teams out of the group, and one team has to prove that SUD is a disease and the other team has to prove that it is not. There is a judge and jury, and they go by the same protocol as in court.

o   <u>Trauma Related</u>: Ask clients, who have experienced trauma (which may be all the members of an SUD group), where and with whom they currently feel safe, "warm," and loved, and how they have lived with feeling unsafe and unloved in the past. Also ask them that when a trauma is triggered during a group session, that they: remind themselves that "Nothing bad is happening right now."; be gentle with themselves and ask the group to be gentle with them; and talk with them about how they may work with the trauma when it is triggered outside the group (e.g., sit in the sunshine).

o   <u>Using Versus Recovering Descriptions</u>: Ask group members to divide a sheet of paper in half and write "using" on one side and "recovering" on the other. Then ask them to write down as many characteristics about themselves as they can under these columns: how they are when they're using or how people have told them they are when they're using, and then have them do the same for the recovery column. Ask each person to contribute one or two of the items they have written down under each category.

o   <u>Vacuum of Recovery</u>: Have clients make a list on paper of things they don't need in their lives anymore on half a sheet of paper. On the other half, have them write down what they would like to put in the space they have created within themselves by throwing away the things they didn't need anymore: What would they like to replace those things with? Then go outside and do a burning ritual where they set that piece of paper of things they don't need any more on fire. Have them process in group their reactions to the burning and what they have left on their remaining sheet of paper. <u>Note</u>: This is also known in SUD recovery as "people, places, things" (the terminology may vary) that need to be changed.

O   <u>Whole Person Wheel Drawing</u>: Have each client draw a circle and divide it into different parts, such as physical, mental, emotional, spiritual, etc. Group members can use the wheel to discuss the various aspects of themselves in their recovery process.

FAMILY/RELATIONSHIPS/CULTURE

These are exercises or role-playing games that explore family, relationship, and cultural dynamics.

Family

In Person Only (with Family Members)

O   <u>Baby Book Therapy</u>: Ask parents to go home and review their child's baby books. In the following session, discuss their positive memories of the child.

O   <u>Grief Over Child's Usage</u>: Have parents bring in a baby picture of their child and think about that picture. Usually this will get good thoughts going on in their heads and then bring them back to why they are here (their child is in treatment). Have them look at their child and ask them, "Did you ever envision being in this setting, at this time, with this problem?" Of course, they generally answer, "No." As they're reflecting back on the picture, talk about each stage of grief and how it relates to their child and their own personal feelings. It helps them understand where they are in the stages of grief and how all of those stages have affected them. It also helps them to understand that they are angry with their child for what they've done.

O   <u>Impact of the SUD on the Family</u>: Have the group get into a circle while the family members stay on the outside of the circle. Ask the family members to listen, and have the group talk about how their active SUD affected their relationships with their family members. After they complete this, the family members get on the inside of the circle and the group members get on the outside of the circle, and the family members talk about how the SUD of their loved ones affected them. Then, have everyone get into a common circle and process. Some of the family members will have had no idea what some of their loved ones were going through, and the clients get to hear about some of the things they were doing to their family members.

O <u>Mirroring</u>: One family member is the listener and one is the sender. They sit face-to-face and one tells the other something that it is difficult to talk about in very short phrases, short enough so the other person can remember what is said. The listener is to reflect back, as a mirror, saying, "I hear you say there's something you want me to talk to you about," and this continues as specifics are given on the listener's alcohol and drug use (e.g., "You know that time on Christmas Eve when you got drunk?" "That time on Christmas Eve when I got drunk."). It has to be structured very tightly, and the counselor's job is to make sure that the person who is listening says back exactly what they hear, rather than what they have interpreted or understood, and that the sender is speaking in short enough phrases that the listener can repeat them. Each time after the sender says a phrase, the listener repeats it and says, "Is that right and is there more?" This continues until the sender has no more to say and then the roles for the family member and the client are reversed.

In Person/Online

O <u>Family Constellation with the Victim</u>: Have the SUD client set up the scene with their choice of a group member, who is willing to act as the perpetrator, and group members, who are willing to act as other members of their family constellation. Have all the group members stand around the circle of the family constellation. Carefully process the family constellation trauma as the client is willing to go through it: first focus on the client's thinking, then the client's emotions, and finally, have the client state beliefs about themselves that emerged as a result of the trauma. Ask them how they would like to change those beliefs about themselves, and write those changed beliefs on a card that they read both to the family constellation and the group members witnessing the family constellation experience.

(Note: This exercise can also be used for any relationship that is experiencing conflict both within and outside the group. In such a role play, the SUD client can say, "When you _____________, I felt this, and it reminds me of _____________"; possibly something from their childhood or a family experience memory. Then have them tell the other person what they want that person to do differently, and state what they need to do differently. The whole group then processes what happened and affirms the SUD client who went through the experience.)

O <u>Family Dinner Table</u>: Have group members draw their dinner tables and where everybody sits during dinnertime. This can lead to discussions about family dynamics, the importance of family and unity, isolation issues, etc. <u>Caution</u>: The larger the group, the more cumbersome it may be to process member reactions.

O <u>Family Dynamics</u>: Have each client draw a diagram of how he or she remembers his or her family doing something, like being at dinner or the playground or a relative's house. Family can refer to a mother and father or to an aunt, siblings—whatever family is to that person. Afterward, go over the diagram and discuss what the client sees in the picture and what the counselor sees in the picture. For example, the client may draw the siblings farther away from everyone else or draw the mother smaller than the father, etc. This can lead to a discussion about family dynamics and also about connecting family dynamics from the past to the present. <u>Caution</u>: This exercise may work better in a group that is cohesive.

O <u>Family Sculpture</u>: First, identify the different roles in a SUD family (e.g., SUD client, chief enabler, hero, scapegoat, lost child, mascot) and have group members volunteer to play the different roles in the chosen SUD client's family. The sculpture can be done a couple of different ways: (1) do a generic family sculpture where group members, chosen by the client, represent the different roles with the client placing their bodies in the position that represents their role in relation to the client and then have another group member act as an observer who goes around the sculpture observing and/or asking questions of the group members in the roles or (2) ask for a volunteer to sculpt their own family of origin and then ask for volunteers to play the different roles in their family. Clients may not know what to do with the flood of emotions that the exercise can bring on, so for both options, process the activity after the sculpting.

○ <u>Family Treatment Progress</u>: Have group members write down and describe what their family is like at the beginning of treatment ("What do we need to change?" "What do we do to achieve that?"). Hold on to these comments until the end of their SUD treatment and have them review that description again ("What have we accomplished?") and process with the group.

○ <u>Hollywood Movies</u>: Use a movie and break it into three sections: (1) the building of the SUD, (2) the SUD treatment program, and (3) the SUD recovery. Process the family dynamics operating in each section.

○ <u>Mock Funeral</u>: Do a role-play of an SUD client's funeral with group members playing the religious official as well as members of the "deceased's" family of origin. Have them gather around the body and have the client (they shouldn't speak) observe their own funeral. After the service is finished, everybody says their farewell, and the group can process the exercise to see what effect this has had on the client.

Relationships

In Person Only

○ <u>Desk Assistance</u>: Have the shortest person in the group stand on a desk. Then ask the tallest person to stand on the floor next to the desk. The person on the desk is supposed to help the person on the floor get onto the desk, and they are able to do this because they can work together.

Then ask them to repeat the exercise, but this time the person on the floor is told to not cooperate. This exercise demonstrates the fact that clients need to be very careful about their own recovery (e.g., shortest person) when helping a friend (e.g., tallest person) with theirs. <u>Caution</u>: Be sensitive to mobility issues with clients that may exclude them from participation.

In Person/Online

○ <u>Impact of SUD on Significant Other Visualization</u>: Have everyone close their eyes and think about one special person whom they love very much. Then have them open their eyes and talk in group about how this special person was specifically impacted by their SUD and how it has affected their relationship with that person. This helps them to see how their SUD became more important than the relationship with that person they loved and that that is how powerful disease is.

○ <u>Relationship Concern Index Cards</u>: Have group members write their name on a piece of paper in large letters and decorate it. Then have them use small sticky notes, on which they write the names of the people they are concerned about or fearful for, and place them on their piece of paper. Then process what they see on their piece of paper. Often, they will say things like, "I can't see myself anymore. I have an awful lot of sticky notes on here, an awful lot of people I worry about." This can lead into a discussion about what would happen as they imagine letting go of those people (e.g., not worrying about them).

○ <u>Significant Other Letter</u>: Tell each client to write a letter to themselves as a significant other would write them a letter. The letter tells them 15 specific examples of how the client hurt others as a result of their SUD. The letter is sealed and not read until the client's assigned time to share it in group. If a group member is adamant that they do not have anyone who would write them a letter, the group members can tell the client or write a letter to the client as they would imagine someone would have written the client a letter.

○ <u>Transactional Analysis Exercise</u>: This exercise can result in a discussion regarding the client's behavior in the context of the group as well as discussion of how they interact with others outside the group. In this exercise, use the visual diagram (Figure 3.2) and explain the model to clients as follows. *First*, explain that ***"P"*** = Parent; ***"A"*** = Adult; ***"C"*** = Child. Tell them that metaphorically: (1) every human being has these 3-cylinder parts inside themselves, (2) each person in the group is a cylinder (e.g., counselor; client) that has these 3 parts, and (3) every person they relate to in their interactions outside the group also has these 3 parts. *Second*, in terms of interactions with others, Person 1 (the ***first cylinder***) is the **client** and Person 2 (the ***second cylinder***) is the **other person** (e.g., counselor; group members; people they interact with outside the group). *Third*, clients need to learn

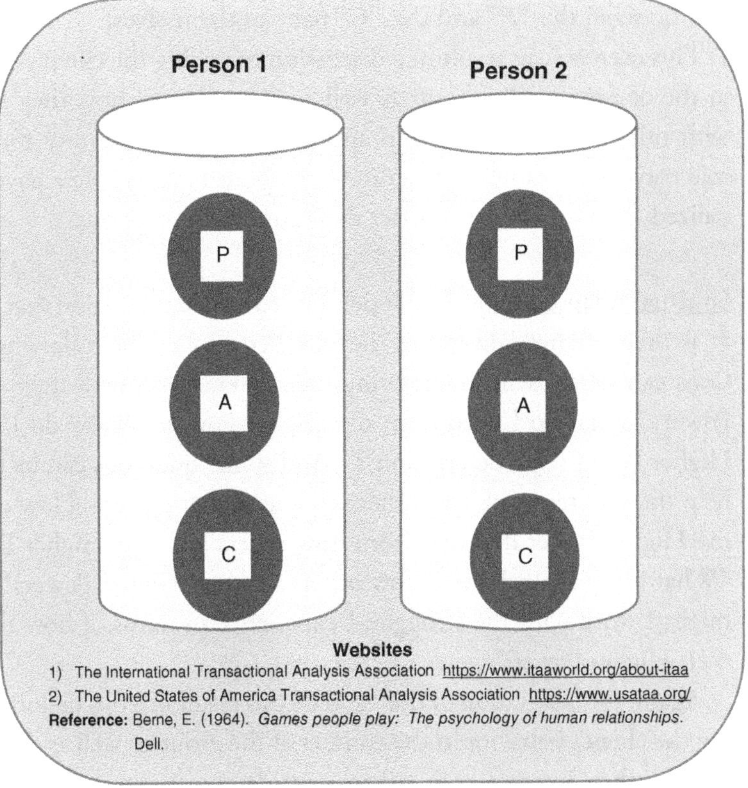

Figure 3.2 Transactional Analysis (TA). *Source*: Miller (2024). Academic violence and bullying of faculty. Cognella Inc.

how these 3 parts interact within themselves so they can be more self-aware and have improved interactions with others. *Finally*, they need to understand what happens in an ideal interaction with another person as well as possible realistic interactions with others. In the *ideal interaction*, the client stays in the *"A"* mode (e.g., calm, clear, honest, genuine) in order to invite an *"A"* mode response (e.g., calm, clear, honest, genuine) in the other person. In possible *realistic interactions*, the client may be pulled into a *"P"* mode (e.g., a critical parent OR a rescuing parent) by the other person's *"C"* mode behavior (e.g., a rebellious child OR a helpless child) or the reverse (a *"C"* mode response [e.g., a rebellious child OR a helpless child] by the other person's *"P"* mode behavior).

Note that this exercise can also be explained to clients as follows: the *"P"* is the cognitive part of themselves, the *"C"* is the emotional part of themselves and the *"A"* is the part of themselves that serves as the mediator between the *"P"* and the *"C"* parts of themselves.

This exercise can result in a discussion regarding the client's behavior in the context of the group as well as discussion of how they interact with others outside the group and provide an opportunity for group role plays. For example, they can learn about messages they have internalized from others that impact their current interactions.

○ <u>Spiritual Adaptation of the Model</u>: Have the client imagine that Person #1 is their Higher Power and they are Person #2. The following questions can assist them in exploring their interactions with their Higher Power: "What do I need from my Higher Power?" "How do I see my Higher Power (e.g., description)?". Additional questions can be used to help them in terms of how others view a Higher Power: "How do I see my Higher Power different from how others see their Higher Power?" "What is my struggle with how others see their Higher Power?" "How might I work with the struggles I experience in terms of how they see their Higher Power?"

Again, the adaptation of this exercise can result in a discussion regarding the client's behavior in the context of the group as well as discussion of how they interact with others outside the group and provide an opportunity for group role plays. <u>Caution</u>: The first version can draw out transference (projection) issues with others that may be emotionally powerful and specifically with the spiritual adaptation, issues the client has with the concept of a Higher Power.

Culture

In Person Only

○ <u>Sharing Culture</u>: Have the group members get into a large circle in order to talk about what everyone wants to share with each other from their culture. The first person is given a ball of yarn, holds onto a piece of the yarn, and throws the ball to another person, saying, "This is my gift to you, I want to share this." Then that person holds a piece of the yarn and throws the ball to someone else and shares something. By the end of the exercise, the yarn is all used, and it looks like a spider web. Have the group process the interconnectedness of people as well as our uniqueness.

In Person/Online

○ <u>Acculturation Process (for clients from a country other than the United States)</u>: Tell them that the room is a map and ask them to indicate where their native country is and where the United States is. Then tell them, "Go ahead and stand in this map where you were 10 years ago." Then say, "Go to the place in the map where you were five years ago." Then say, "Go stand where you have been in the last year." Finally tell them, "Go and stand in the place where everything would be perfect and where you would love to live. Where is your heart, where is your passion?" Lastly say, "Go stand in the place where the person you love the most, the person who is the most important to you, is right now,". Process client reactions to the exercise.

(<u>Note</u>: Another version of this exercise could be adjusting it to different places in the United States or within the state where group members are receiving treatment. Such an adjustment would allow all group members to participate and highlight the different cultural experiences of group members.)

(<u>Also note</u>: Both versions of this exercise can be adapted to online groups by having members draw the map out on a piece of paper.)

FEELINGS EXPLORATION

These are exercises that help clients identify feelings.

In Person Only

○ <u>Discussion of Fear</u>: Give each client three pieces of paper. Ask them to write on each piece of paper what their fears are. After they write one fear on each piece, they crumple up each piece of paper into a snowball. Then they all have to throw their snowballs at each other on the count of three. They can throw them at anybody, but they cannot throw all three of their papers at the same person. Everybody has to pick up the snowball closest to them and then go around the room and read the fear that someone else wrote about. Encourage them to talk about whether they identify with that fear and whether they can identify who the fear belonged to.

○ <u>Feelings Bowl</u>: Take a bowl with feelings words written on paper in it and have each group member draw one out. Then have them each describe a scene that comes to their minds when they think of the word and how it relates to their lives.

○ <u>Feelings Cards</u>: Write down various feelings on index cards (e.g., anger, guilt, loneliness), and then pass out the cards to various members and have them share experiences related to their childhood, teen years, and adult years that connect to the feelings card they draw.

○ <u>Human Being Pillow</u>: Take a pillow and tell the group to imagine that the words "I am a human being" are written on the pillow. Toss the pillow to one of the more talkative group members and ask them to share something they feel. When they are done, have them toss the pillow to someone else to share their feelings while they say, "Remember, you are a human being too."

○ <u>"Shoulds"</u>: Have the clients write down "shoulds" on a sheet of paper, such as, "I should be married, because I'm 40 years old," or "I should have a family," Then have them write down the "shoulds" they feel comfortable letting go of. They have to write them down on small pieces of paper they tape them to helium-filled balloons that are taken outside. Ask them, "Are you ready to let go of this thing that's holding you back?" and if they are ready, tell them they can release their balloon. If they're not, then they have to hold onto the balloon.

In Person/Online

○ <u>Body Awareness 1</u>: If a client has a feeling that they cannot name, it can be helpful to ask him/her where the feeling is in their body. If they answer, "It's like a fist in my throat," or "It's like a ball in my stomach," you can ask them to describe it: what it feels like, looks like, and what is its shape and size. Once the client begins to talk about what the problem is in terms of their body, you can work together on it through imagery. For example, if a client says their heart is as cold as ice, ask, "Would you like to get it warmer? Would you like to change it?" and if so, ask, "How would you want to warm up your heart?" The client may respond, "I guess I put a blanket around it," and the counselor can say, "Well, then get a blanket and put it around your heart." Then process the thoughts and feelings with the experience. <u>Caution</u>: For trans or nonbinary clients, this exercise can add an additional layer of challenge so it may be helpful to be cautious in the use of this exercise. <u>Note</u>: This exercise may be paired with progressive muscle relaxation.

○ <u>Body Awareness 2</u>: Ask everybody to freeze their facial expression and body language and then answer the question, "What would your facial expression say if it could talk for you?" They may say things like, "If my facial expression could talk it would say, 'I'm really annoyed with that person over there,'" or, "I really don't want to be in group today," or, "I'm really hopeful that we can talk about this or that." <u>Caution</u>: For trans or nonbinary clients, this exercise can add an additional layer of challenge so it may be helpful to be cautious in the use of this exercise. <u>Note</u>: This exercise may be paired with progressive muscle relaxation.

○ <u>Cognitive-Behavioral Triangle</u>: Have clients talk about behaviors they have engaged in or feelings they have had, and they can use the triangle to connect their behavior to their feelings and their thoughts. This can help illustrate that behavior can change based on what one is feeling and that if feelings and thoughts are changed, behavior can also be changed.

○ <u>Emotional Description</u>: Get a person to describe what emotion they're feeling at the moment and talk about that. Ask the group to respond about what emotions they feel as the other person is talking. Draw commonality among the members by talking about what everyone is feeling at that time.

○ <u>Emotional Disclosure ("A Matter of Concern")</u>: Have everybody write their name on the top of a sheet of paper followed by a matter of emotional concern. It can be very brief: "I'm angry at my wife." "I'm sad because my dog died." Have them turn the paper into the counselor. Then have some group members choose other group members to act as their counselors. The "client" group member will tell the "counselor" group member what is going on, and the "counselor" will give them feedback, so there is a one-on-one inside the group.

○ <u>Feelings Chart</u>: Use a large, colorful feeling and emotion words chart (or draw one on a board). Have a client pick one of the feelings or emotions that they are experiencing that day and process it. Then have the other group members discuss how they feel in response to what the client said.

○ <u>Half Smile</u>: Ask each member of the group to identify a person that they really dislike or hate. Then ask the members to close their eyes, put a half smile on their face, and continue to smile throughout the whole episode. Then ask them, while they have their eyes closed and they're smiling, to picture the person they dislike and to think about what it is they dislike/hate most about them. Then ask, "What is it like to be this person? What do you think motivates them to act the way they do?" as well as any other improvised questions. Lastly, ask them to think about how they envision this person now. Then all of the members open their eyes and the group processes each member's reaction to the exercise.

○ "I Take Responsibility": Have each group member state the emotion that they have at that time and state that they take responsibility for it. For example, "I'm angry today and I take responsibility for it."

○ Leader Pose: The counselor asks everybody to close their eyes and then strikes a pose. When they open their eyes, they look at the counselor (who is standing on a chair, crossing their arms, staring down at them, etc.) and process how they feel: Does the counselor's pose remind them of any person or experience from their past?

○ Military Metaphor: Ask members to use the different branches of service to describe how they are feeling.

○ Object Projection: If someone is having trouble expressing their feelings, it can be useful to give them some sort of inanimate object, such as a ball or a pen, and have them project themselves onto that object and describe what the pen or the ball is feeling. This helps them to describe their feelings indirectly through metaphor.

○ T-Shirt/Sweatshirt: Have group members draw a T-shirt or undershirt on a piece of paper. On that shirt have them write feelings about things that they have done that they don't want anyone to know about. Then on a separate sheet of paper, have them draw a sweatshirt that represents what they want to project to the world. This exercise helps them talk about feelings more and explore the two different "shirts."

○ The Supermarket: Have the group members imagine that they are in a supermarket where they are to pick up an item they would like to be and put it inside a bag—they also choose other items they put in the bag. Each group member imagines themselves to be the item that they placed in the bag. Ask them what they are in the bag, why they choose to be that item, and what other items are in the bag with them and the location of that item. For example, if someone says that they are a loaf of bread and there is a ham sitting on top of them, ask them how they feel about that. If somebody says they are a dozen eggs, it might signal that they are feeling fragile and important to ask them how the other items in the bag may crack or break them. If someone says they are a six-pack of soda pop in the bottom of the bag as well as other items, it may signal that they feel they are carrying a lot of "weight" in their bag that they need to process in group.

o   <u>Toys/Stuffed Animals</u>: Have clients pick a toy or stuffed animal that describes how they feel that day as they enter group. They then explain why they feel like that toy or stuffed animal today.

o   <u>Water Bowl</u>: Take a bowl of water and put it in the middle of the room. Give each client a cup to dip into the water, not knowing what they are going to do with it. Have them stand in a circle around the water and go around the room, starting with the counselor, and say, "What I'm thirsting for today is ________________."

GROUP COMMUNITY BUILDING

These exercises help promote group cohesion and/or help group members discover that they have things in common with each other.

In Person Only

o   <u>Group as a Mirror</u>: With a group that has met a few times, have some of the group members sit in a circle and have the rest of the group members sit outside of the circle. Then conduct ½ of the group time with the members in the circle and let the members sitting outside the circle observe. This can act as a healing exercise and can also help the observers identify with things that they may not have in previous groups. Then switch the group members (inside and outside the group) and repeat the process.

o   <u>Hula Hoop Balance</u>: Group members stand in a circle where each member holds out one of their fingers and a hula hoop is placed on the group members' fingers. They begin by holding the hoop at a certain level and then bringing it down to the floor and then back up again without the hoop falling. This exercise can be done in silence or with group members talking with one another. Then process the group members' reactions to the experience (Figure 3.3).

Figure 3.3　Geri Miller, Ph.D. *SUD Group Counseling Hulahooping Technique Demonstration.*
February 2025 NCFADS Winter School Workshop Break.
Source: Courtesy of Michael Roberts.

○　<u>Hula Hoop Pass</u>: Have members form a circle where one member holds onto a hula hoop with one hand. Members then pass the hula hoop to one another, but they continue to hold the hula hoop until all members are holding it. Then process the experience with the group.

○　<u>Musical Chairs</u>: Play musical chairs for about 30 minutes and then process what the group members have seen in each other. Group members tend to show childhood behaviors.

○　<u>Nonmusical Chairs</u>: Have one chair less in the group than the number of group members. Ask group members to sit down, and the person left standing goes to the middle of the circle and says something personal about themselves and then states something like, "Anyone who has a name starting with an A come to the middle." That person exchanges places with the person in the middle. This continues until everyone in the group has the opportunity to be in the middle of the circle and share personal information.

O   <u>Positive Feedback</u>: Have clients write their names on a piece of paper and then tape the papers to the back of each client. Have each client write one positive strength that they see in that individual on the piece of paper; have them do this for each group member. Stress that everybody has a positive strength that each member can write down for other members.

O   <u>Santa</u>: Use a small stuffed teddy bear called "Santa," and do not let group members talk until they have Santa in their hands. If they would like to talk, then they have to raise their hand in order to get Santa. If someone has Santa and somebody else wants him, the person who has him can hold onto him until they have finished what they have to say.

O   <u>Stereotype Line</u>: Ask for five volunteers and arrange them in a line. Pick one member out of the group and have them organize everybody according to their age—from youngest to oldest—and plug themselves in where they think they belong. They cannot ask the people their age. Have each person try to do this. Afterward, find out who was right (or most right). Then discuss how we cannot judge a book by its cover.

In Person/Online

O   <u>Courtroom</u>: When new clients come into group, have it set up like a courtroom: the experienced group members are the jury, district attorney, and defense attorney (representing the new client), and the leader is the judge. Each new client introduces oneself, one's drug of choice, number of treatments, and how seriously they are taking treatment. The jury, district attorney, and judge all pretend to get to decide whether or not the new client can come into the group and decide what issues need to be addressed. While the counselor makes the final decision, everybody has input, and the group works together collaboratively to find ways to include the member—all new members are accepted into the group. The exercise helps create a cohesiveness and unity within the group and helps everybody get to know each other.

○ <u>Criminal Issues</u>: Ask what criminal issues group members are struggling with at that time, discuss them, and process feedback they receive from their peers.

○ <u>Emotional Bonding</u>: Have group members introduce themselves on a first-name basis and share a little bit about themselves. Have them share a feeling and emotion that they are experiencing at that time. After that brief introduction, ask the group to point out the members they are most concerned about.

○ <u>Group Member Evaluation</u>: Have group members who know each other well evaluate each other about how they are doing in their recovery. Sometimes this creates a lot of positive interaction, although occasionally it creates confrontation.

○ <u>Johari Window</u>: Use this visual image (Figure 3.4) to assist clients in understanding what they are doing in group therapy: they are learning about their blind quadrant, hidden quadrant, and unknown quadrant through group community feedback. This feedback helps them develop their capacity to be more open in their interactions if they choose to be. It assists with group community building because members can learn how to more effectively interact with others in the group.

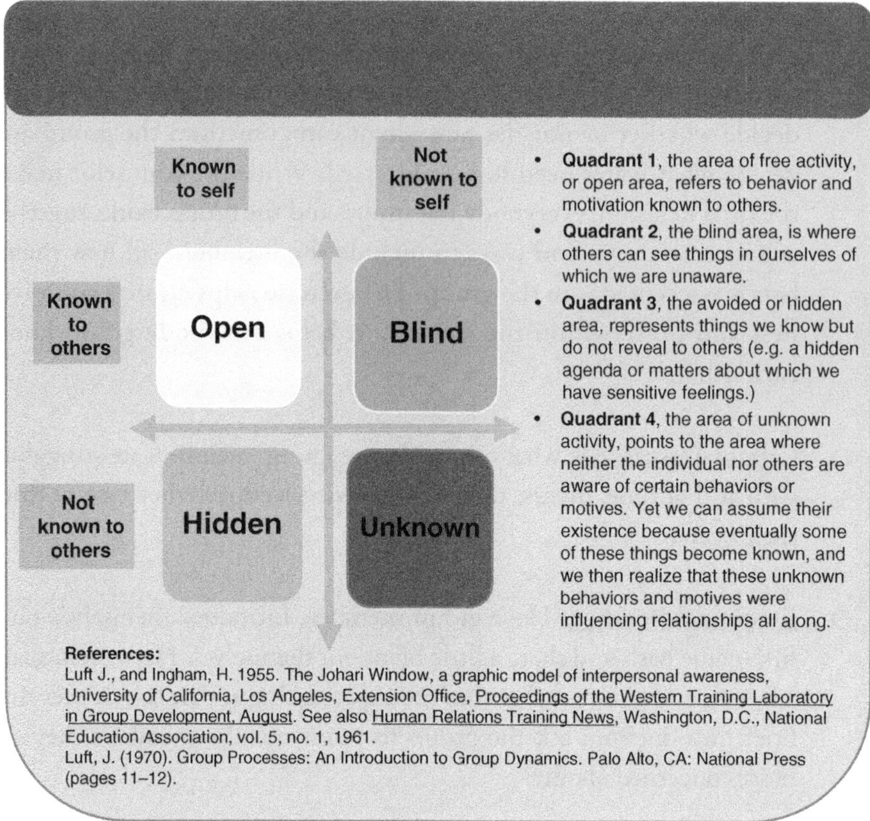

Figure 3.4   The Johari window (Luft, 1970; Luft and Ingham, 1955).
Source: Miller (2024). Academic violence and bullying of faculty. Cognella Inc.

<u>Suggestions</u>: Explain the quadrants to the group by inserting in each quadrant the statements "I know" [what the group member knows about themselves] and "You don't know" [what the other members/leader know about them]. The statements that inserted in each of the quadrants are as follows:

Open: "I know" "You know"

Blind: "I don't know" "You know"

Hidden: "I know" "You don't know"

Unknown: "I don't know" "You don't know"

This simple explanation of the Johari Window quadrants can assist group members in (1) understanding the quadrants; (2) learning how group feedback can help them learn about themselves (e.g., how they can "decrease" their blind quadrant of "I don't know" by hearing what other members know about them); and (3) facilitating discussion of their boundaries with others (e.g., how the hidden quadrant determines what they want others to know about them).

Avoid the tendency of clients to be superficial by asking them questions such as: "What have you told the group about your SUD behavior?" (*open quadrant*) "What feedback have you received from others outside this group about your SUD behavior—feedback that you do not understand or agree with?" (*blind quadrant*); "What keeps you from sharing hidden aspects of yourself with the group?" (*hidden quadrant*); "As you continue in the group, you will learn more about yourself— what fears do you have about learning more about yourself?" (*unknown quadrant*)

O <u>Leader Modeling</u>: Turn the group over to one of the group members. The member of the group who is leading the group tries to emulate the counselor.

SELF-ESTEEM

These are exercises that help clients work on their self-esteem.

In Person Only

O <u>Compliment Exchange</u>: Have a group member turn to the person to their left and give that person a compliment. Have each member do this in turn until everyone in the group has received a compliment. Then have a group member start the same process with the person to their right until everybody in this direction has received a compliment. Afterward, the group processes and discusses whether they had difficulty giving or receiving a compliment. <u>Caution</u>: Trans and/or nonbinary members may be tired of hearing compliments such as "You are so brave" and may need to be encouraged to express how they feel about compliments that have been given to them by other group members. <u>Suggestion</u>: The leader may need to encourage members to avoid focusing on physical appearance and instead focus on what they contribute to the group.

O <u>Group Member Positive Feedback</u>: The group forms a circle and one person will pick another person, stand in front of them, look them in the eye, and tell them what kind of positive changes and growth they have seen in that person since they came to treatment. Once everyone has had a turn, process how they felt giving people compliments, getting compliments, and having to stand there and accept the compliment without saying "No, No." <u>Caution</u>: Trans and/or nonbinary members may be tired of hearing compliments such as "You are so brave" and may need to be encouraged to express how they feel about compliments that have been given to them by other group members.

In Person/Online

O <u>Admired People</u>: Ask the group members to name three to five people that they admire and put down two adjectives that describe why they admire those people. Process the experience by focusing on the clients' description of these people reflecting who they are as people. An additional component is to have them circle the adjectives that are the same or similar, thereby reflecting the client's values. <u>Note</u>: This can be adapted to include fictional characters they admire. Also, whether real or fictional, this exercise can lead to a discussion of values.

O <u>I Am</u>: Have the group members think of all the things they enjoy doing in life besides alcohol and drugs. Then ask them to write out every single thing they can think of, starting with "I am." So, it may be "I am music; I am laughter; I am a rainy day with raindrops touching my tongue; I am running through the mountains; I am driving down the highway with my window down." Ask for volunteers to share some of what they have written. Ask them what they wrote that was positive. <u>Note</u>: This can assist members as viewing themselves as more than a person in SUD recovery.

O <u>Letter to a Teenager</u>: Have group members write a letter to a teenager that they love. It can be a younger brother, sister, niece, or nephew or just somebody they knew in their neighborhood growing up. They should write the letter to the teenager as if the teenager were leaving them in the next week to go out into the world as an adult. The letter should be about what they hope and wish for the teenager. They should also include in that letter something about what they hope and wish for them in terms of their alcohol and drug use in the future. Then ask them to share their letters, if they wish, and discuss how *they* deserved the experience that they are wishing for this other person that they love, and how they need to treat themselves with this same kind of love and hope for the future as they would have for the teenager.

O <u>Lifeboat</u>: Divide the group into smaller groups and tell them that each group has a lifeboat, but the lifeboat will only fit all but one of them (e.g., if the group is five people, the lifeboat can only hold four). The group members have to talk about why they are valuable and why they should be allowed to get on the boat. They also need to talk about how hurtful it is to the person to be left out of the boat just as it is for a person to be left out of the group. Help them talk about ways to keep everyone in the group.

O <u>Mirror Talk</u>: In a group session, have clients plan on three times a day for two minutes each, stand in front of a mirror and say three positive things about themselves. During this time, there is to be no brushing teeth or combing hair or taking care of cosmetic needs. This time is strictly to look in the mirror. When the three positives have been spoken, the client is to continue looking in the mirror for the full two minutes. Have them process this experience in the next group.

O <u>Nature Association</u>: Ask clients to identify themselves with something in nature (e.g., tree, stream, animal), and then have them describe the importance of that aspect of nature and why it is important to the world. Talk about how unique and important each one of those things is to nature and how the clients are also unique and important to human society.

O <u>Self-Inventory</u>: Have group members write down five things they like about themselves and five things they don't like about themselves and process what they write.

RECOVERY SKILLS: COMMUNICATION/MINDFULNESS/ PROBLEM SOLVING

These exercises are meant to assist clients in developing these recovery skills.

Communication

In Person/Online

O <u>"I" Statement Leader Modeling</u>: The leader says to the group, "For the next 30 minutes, I am going to model 'I' statements. If any of you catch me using anything other than 'I' statements, point it out to me, and the first one to point it out to me will get [some type of reward]." This exercise (1) models "I" statements for the group; (2) helps members be attentive to what is being said; and (3) holds the leader accountable to the group and therefore models accountability for them.

Mindfulness

In Person Only

○ <u>Outdoor Items</u>: Bring natural outdoor things into group (e.g., flowers, rocks, petals). Start group by having each person hold one of these natural objects in their hands for a two- or three-minute meditation. Have them concentrate on that object—smelling it, touching it, turning it over, looking at it.

○ <u>Outdoor Meditation</u>: Have the group meditate outside. Tell them, "Don't really look at anything in particular. Allow yourself to see everything at once and be in the moment, because the objective is to look out and notice that you can see movement and things happening."

In Person/Online

○ <u>Candy</u>: Have members unwrap a piece of candy, smell it, feel the texture in their mouth, and slowly taste it.

○ <u>Guided Imagery</u>: Open group with a guided imagery, such as a meditation, and have everyone work on breathing and feeling where their stress is inside of their bodies and how they can work with that stress.

Problem Solving

In Person Only

○ <u>Rock Painting</u>: Bring rocks to group and let members choose the size of their rocks and paint on them the problem they are facing in their recovery. After painting the rocks, they have to hold their rocks until they come up with a reasonable working solution to solve their problems. Process how the rock symbolizes their struggle in recovery.

In Person/Online

O   <u>Monday Writing</u>: Write the word "Monday" on the board in cursive with all the letters connected. Then say, "Is there a way you can write Monday, without connecting the M or the O, and without the pen ever leaving the paper or the board?" The group members will say, "No, that can't be done." However, it can be done. Instead of starting with the letter M, start writing the word "Monday" with the letter O and write "O-N-D-A-Y" and continue the Y to the beginning of the word and add in the M, and the word is written in cursive, without connecting the M and the O.

O   <u>Nine Dots Puzzle</u>: Draw nine dots that form a square (three lines of three dots each). Put a client's name at the top of the square. Ask the client, "How can you make your life come together? If these nine dots represented your life and you had to connect all nine dots with four straight lines, is there a way that you could do that?" Generally, the group members will say that there is no way to do it. However, it can be done by going, literally, outside of the box. Starting at the top left-hand corner, draw a diagonal line to the bottom right-hand corner. Then, draw a line straight up to the top right-hand corner, but then keep going outside the square for a little distance, and come back diagonally to the middle left-hand dot. Keep going outside of the box until you can draw a straight line through the bottom line of dots. By going outside the box, you can connect all nine dots. This exercise can be used to demonstrate that things are possible, that sometimes somebody can help show you how to put your life together, and that sometimes you have to think "outside the box."

O   <u>Solution Exploration</u>: Have the group process the issue a client brings up for discussion and let the group come up with the solution(s).

O   <u>Using Triggers</u>: Have a group member identify a substance abuse trigger, and have them walk the leader through five strategies that they have developed to help them deal with that trigger.

VALUES

These exercises are intended to assist clients in clarifying their values and more useful in smaller rather than larger groups.

In Person/Online

○ <u>Airplane/Lifeboat Story</u>: Tell the group a story about a plane that crashes with 12 people on it and that there is a lifeboat, but it can only hold 6 people. Give the group a list of the 12 people on the plane with brief descriptions of them that you have paired with a value that you do not share with the group. For example, 1 passenger is 6 years old—this person is paired with the value of children. Each group member has to decide on the 6 individuals they choose and why. Then the entire group needs to discuss/debate which 6 individuals they believe need to be on the boat and why. After the activity, have each member choose their top five values from a values list and number them 1 (most important) to 5 (least important). Then discuss how their current behaviors align (or don't align) with their values.

○ <u>Drawbridge Exercise</u>: Tell the group the story of a lady who is married to a nobleman. The nobleman leaves the castle and warns the lady that if she leaves, she'll experience a dire consequence. She leaves and visits her lover in the village and upon returning finds a madman at the gate of the drawbridge. The madman warns her that if she tries to cross, he will kill her. She goes back to the village to try to get help. She first goes to the lover, who tells her he wants nothing to do with it; she then goes to her best friend, who says she doesn't want anything to do with it because she shouldn't have disobeyed her husband; and then she goes to a boatman, who just wants money. Ultimately, she decides to cross the drawbridge and is killed. The group then tries to determine who is responsible for her death, which elicits a discussion of values and consequences of actions.

○ <u>Desert Island Story</u>: Tell a story about 2 people from the United States who are stranded on a desert island. One person has a disease and has to take medicine every six hours—there is only enough medicine available for one dose. They have one gun and one bullet left. A 3rd person comes to the island in a boat, is hungry, and has no food. The person who does not need the medicine tells the new arrival of their situation, and the new arrival says, "If you have sex with me, I will take you back to the United States, but there is only room for two people in my boat." After they hear the story, members are to write down how they would resolve the situation. They are only given three to four minutes. Then, as a group, they have 15 minutes to come to a mutual decision about how to solve the problem and they all have to agree. At the end of 15 minutes (regardless of whether the group has come to a decision) process the decision-making process (e.g., how decisions were made, contributing values) with the group.

○ <u>Value Clarification</u>: Have each group member write down four items that they value. Then have them remove one item out of the four that is least valuable to them. Have them repeat this process until all of the items are gone. Use this exercise to have group members explore what is important to them and to explore the idea that if they relapse, they may lose these important items.

○ <u>What's Important to Me?</u>: Ask the group: "If I was all-powerful and came to you and told you that in 20 minutes you had to move to an unknown destination, and you could pick three things to take with you on this journey (it cannot be a person), what three things would you take with you?" Then process the clients' answers.

OPENERS

Opening Statements

- "Please introduce yourself in this way: 'I am . I work at .'"
- "How did everyone get into this group? If you were referred, how did you get referred?"
- "How is everyone doing today?"
- "Is there anything you need to talk about today?"
- "What do we need to do today?"
- "What do you want to work on today?"
- "If everything was perfect in your life, what would your life be like?"
- "How is your family coping with your SUD treatment?"
- "Any leftovers from our prior group?"

General Opening Activities

In Person Only

- Make contact with each person (handshake/speak to them) before group begins or at the beginning of group.
- Provide snacks and coffee.

In Person/Online

- Have a welcoming tone.
- Be positive and encouraging.
- Introduce self and opening exercise.
- Do name introductions and review group norms (e.g., interpersonal safety, confidentiality).
- Ask members to take one to three minutes to get ready/think about what to use group for and how they feel.
- Read daily devotional reading.
- Do a check-in: spiritually, mentally, emotionally, physically.
- Discuss sobriety time, talk about what members want to get out of group, and how to treat one another in group.
- Ask about goals for that day.
- Introduce a feeling word.
- Discuss accomplishments and challenges ("brags and snags").
- Ask if anyone has a concern they want to discuss.
- Have a longer-term member introduce a topic.
- Identify a high-risk situation for relapse.
- Use humor thoughtfully.
- For a returning group, summarize the previous week's work.
- For a returning group, identify who is going to be absent.

Specific Opening Activities

In Person/Online

- Share your own recovery story with the group thereby opening yourself up to them and modeling how they can open up to the group.
- Have the clients give a self-assessment of how they think they are doing in treatment.

- Check in and find out how everyone's doing and where they are in terms of their recovery. Also, take a moment of silence to recognize the members of the group who are no longer in the group.
- Open a session with a discussion of current events that we in the community have experienced.
- Write an inspirational quote on the board and have the group discuss it.
- Have members close their eyes and focus on their breathing for four deep breaths. Then have them open their eyes and do a check-in by having members tell how they feel about the breathing exercise and coming to the group for treatment.
- Have members go around the group and tell how their day has been and how they are feeling. This helps group members focus and relax in order to concentrate on the topic in group.
- Break the ice with a simple joke (chosen carefully) to help members relax and then give out information about the group's focus for the day.
- Open the group with a daily reading and from that reading pick a topic for that day's group.
- Have group members check in with themselves about where they are spiritually, physically, emotionally, and mentally before group begins.
- Say "Good morning." to an evening group and then ask clients: "If you have a pressing issue, think of something that will help you 'wake up' with regard to that issue in your recovery. What is the issue and what would help you 'wake up'?"
- Open group on Monday, for weeklong groups, by saying, "How is everybody doing?" If something sad or good has happened to them over the weekend, it can be used as the starting point for a conversation.

CLOSERS

Closing Statements

In Person/Online

- "How big is your want to stay sober?"
- "How are you going to remain in recovery 2 more weeks?"
- "What will you do to maintain your sobriety?"
- "What did you learn from our discussion today?"

- ◆ "What do you plan to do with the feedback that the group members have given you?"
- ◆ "Where do we want to go in the next group?"
- ◆ "We're done for today."

General Closing Activities

In Person

- ◆ Give out little cards that say, "Good morning, this is your Higher Power; I will be handling all your problems today," and have them put the cards around their homes.
- ◆ Invite members to be a part of a group hug (allow members to not participate) or place their arms on each other's shoulders (again allowing members to not participate) while in a circle and closing with the serenity prayer or a prayer of their choice.

In Person/Online

- ◆ Read an important segment from a recovery-related text (e.g., Narcotics Anonymous, Alcoholics Anonymous).
- ◆ Have everybody say what they are going to do to prepare for an urge to relapse before they leave group—especially on the last day of group for the week.
- ◆ Give a warning for the time remaining in the group so members can prepare for the ending of the group (e.g., "We are ending the group in 10 minutes.").
- ◆ Make sure everyone feels safe to end group and if they don't, talk with them about how you, as a counselor, and the group can help them feel safe as the group ends for the day.
- ◆ Give homework members can do between now and the next group session.
- ◆ Affirm clients' strengths.
- ◆ Thank people for sharing.
- ◆ Choose the positive statements that each member has said and close on that positive note.
- ◆ Say a prayer of choice, do a one-minute relaxation exercise, and then ask them what they got out of group and what they are going to work on.

- Play music that is soothing.
- Summarize the group's work that day.
- Summarize what went on in group, and allow members to say in a few words what they liked best about what happened in the group.
- Ask the clients to share something they heard in group that day that they had never heard before.
- Ask everyone to say what they are grateful for and what they need from the group before ending.
- Have each member give another member a compliment before ending the group.
- Have group members make a gratitude list so they learn to turn their bad days into good days.
- Have people evaluate the group on a scale of 1 to 10 (10 being the best group experience they have ever had) and discuss their ratings.

Specific Closing Activities
In Person Only

O <u>Graduation Ceremony #1</u>: Give graduates an amethyst stone that they pass around the group, and have each group member tell that person why it was good to have them in group. The member receiving the stone can summarize why the group experience was good for them.

O <u>Graduation Ceremony #2</u>: Have graduates choose a stone with a word like serenity, hope, love, or peace painted on it. When the graduating member chooses a stone, they pass the stone to another group member and each person in the group takes a turn holding that stone and, when holding it, says something positive about that person; something they have appreciated about that person. The facilitator then says goodbye to the graduate.

O <u>Recovery Celebration</u>: Have a group "recovery birthday" party regularly on a specific day of the week or month (e.g., every Thursday; every third Thursday) where everybody brings food. During the party, celebrate the work that group members have done and how many days they have in recovery. Total up everybody's sober time and get a picture of how much recovery is in that room at that moment. Then make a paper chain: (1) have each client write down three strengths in their recovery and three things they feel they're struggling with and share them with the group and (2) have each client's papers clipped together in a chain and keep the chain in the room to symbolize that they are all connected in their strengths and in their struggles.

In Person/Online

○ <u>Certificates</u>: Recognize someone in the group who has done something well—for example, someone who has been honest about a relapse or another difficult situation and has handled it and shared it with the group. Those who have done something noteworthy are presented in group with a certificate with their name on it.

○ <u>Group Feedback to Graduates</u>: Celebrate completion of treatment by asking those people who are completing the treatment program to remain silent for the majority of the group and hear the positive feedback from others. Summarize by asking, "How often have you been in a room where you have heard such positive things?" and also ask the graduates how often they have heard feedback in a loving and caring way as opposed to being put down and their reactions to the positive feedback.

○ <u>Goodbye Group</u>: Ask members who are staying to say goodbye to those leaving and tell something about the people who are leaving: what they like about them, what they learned from them, and what they hope for them.

○ <u>Group Summary</u>: Have someone who has not had the opportunity to say anything in the group to summarize the group experience.

REFERENCES

Berne, E. (1964). *Games people play: The psychology of human relationships*. Dell.

Luft, J. (1970). *Group processes: An introduction to group dynamics*, 11–12. Palo Alto, CA: National Press.

Luft, J. and Ingham, H. (1955). The Johari Window, a graphic model of interpersonal awareness. In: *Proceedings of the Western Training Laboratory in*

Group Development. Los Angeles, Extension Office: University of California, August. See also *Human Relations Training News,* Washington, DC, National Education Association, vol. 5, no. 1, 1961.

Miller, G. (2024). *Substance Use Disorder (SUD) group counseling & group community building: Motivational interviewing focus-Part 2.* Addiction Professionals of North Carolina (APNC).

Ni, C. -F., Lin, C. -C., and DyKeman, C. (2023). Exploring multimodality with online peer-facilitated experiential learning in group work training. *The Journal for Specialists in Group Work 48* (4): 299–316. https://doi.org/10.1080/01933922.2023.2251141.

Okech, J. E. A. (2024). The development and efficacy of group counseling and online group work skills. *The Journal for Specialists in Group Work 49* (2-3): 83–84.

Penarroja, V., Zornoza, A., Orengo, V. et al. (2024). Trust and conflict in online groups with faultlines: Results of an intervention to improve emotion regulation. *The Journal for Specialists in Group Work 49* (2-3): 103–119.

4

Resources

This section is a listing of my personal group counseling favorites in terms of readings, workbooks/exercises, icebreaker card exercises, and websites. These are my personal favorites because I have found them to be pragmatic, useful, succinct, and inviting of group member participation.

The first area, *Current Favorites*, consists of updates from the 1st ed. of this book. This update includes an *emphasis on music therapy* and an *emphasis on the transgender population*. These emphases were chosen because they are of special interest to the author as explained in Section 1. The second area, *Classic Favorites*, are those referenced in the 1st ed. of this book and may be difficult to locate.

CURRENT FAVORITES

READINGS

Readings (Group)

Bieling, P. J., McCabe, R. E., & Antony, M. M. (2022). Cognitive-behavioral therapy in groups. Guilford.

This book is divided into three parts: *Part 1: (General principles of cognitive–behavioral therapy groups)*; *Part 2 (CBT groups for specific populations and presenting problems)*; and *Part 3 (Conclusion)*. In Part 2, there is a chapter on "Substance Use Disorders." In this chapter, the authors present information on how to structure group treatment so clients in recovery can learn to translate behavioral coping skills to real-life situations through skill rehearsal (e.g., presentation of the coping skill; role-play of effective use of the skill; client participation in a behavioral rehearsal role play that allows for skill consolidation and feedback).

Corey, G. (2016). Theory and practice of group counseling (10th ed.). Cengage.

This book has three parts. *Part 1 (Elements of Group Process: An Overview)* has 5 chapters (i.e., introduction to group work; group leadership; ethical and professional issues; early stages of group development; later stages of group development). *Part 2 (Theoretical Approaches to Group Counseling)* has 10 chapters on specific theoretical approaches to group work (i.e., Psychoanalytic Approach; Adlerian Group Counseling; Psychodrama; Existential Approach; Person-Centered Approach; Gestalt Therapy; Cognitive–Behavioral Approaches; Rational Emotive Behavior Therapy; Choice Theory/Reality Therapy; Solution-Focused Brief Therapy and Motivational Interviewing). *Part 3 (Integration and Application)* has 1 chapter (Comparisons, Contrasts, and Integration). It has videos that accompany each chapter.

Ingersoll, K. S., & Wagner, C. C. (2012). Motivational interviewing in groups. Guilford.

This book, while not SUD specific, is an excellent overview of Motivational Interviewing strategies as applied to group counseling.

Yalom, I. D., & Leszcz, M. (2020). The theory and practice of group psychotherapy 6th ed. Basic Books.

This book is based on research and clinical experience. Each chapter is revised to incorporate recent developments in the field. The book has new sections that include online group therapy; interpersonal neurobiology; culture and diversity; and psychological trauma.

Readings (Music)

Gardstrom, S. C. (2021). Music as a trigger for substance abuse. In Gardstrom, S. C., & Willenbrink-Conte, J. (Ed.) (2021). Music therapy with women with addictions (Chapter 18) Barcelona Publishers. Created from wfu on 2022-12-16 20:40:10.

This chapter on cravings focuses on listening to songs as intervention technique. The chapter is anchored in research on music and cravings, clinical experience with a residential female population, and provides talking points on a Trigger worksheet the author developed for a 50-minutes session focusing on the *what, when, where,* and *how* of music listening.

Global Council on Brain Health. (2020). *Music on our minds: The rich potential of music to promote brain health and mental well-being.* www.Global CouncilOnBrainHealth.org; https://doi.org/10.26419/pia.00103.001

This publication discusses the healing power of music through dancing, singing, or movement in order to reduce stress, have physical activity, and socialize.

Silverman, M. J. (2022). Music therapy in mental health for illness management and recovery (2nd ed.). Oxford.

This book, that is both clinically and research based, covers a wide breadth of content. Specific topics of interest related to SUD disorders include a chapter on SUDs that reflect the author's views and an incorporation of "addiction" in each chapter. Each chapter concludes with a "Main Ideas" section that provides the reader with the main points presented in this densely condensed work.

READINGS (SUD CARE)

Substance Abuse and Mental Health Services Administration. (2025). *National guidance on essential specialty substance use disorder (SUD) care* (Publication No. PEP25-04-033). Substance Abuse and Mental Health Services Administration. https://library.samhsa.gov

This publication is a summary of core (e.g., essential services) that need to be available at SUD treatment facilities for adult clients/patients.

Readings (Transgender)

Substance Abuse and Mental Health Services Administration. (2024). *Behavioral health of adolescents across sexual identities: Results from the 2023 National Survey on Drug Use and Health* (SAMHSA Publication No. PEP24-07-028). Center for Behavioral Health Statistics and Quality, Substance Abuse and Mental Health Services Administration. https://www.samhsa.gov/data/report/lgb-adolescent-behavioral-health-2023

This publication highlights the struggles of LGB+ adolescents who continue to have more behavioral health issues in comparison to their heterosexual (straight) peers that include depression, suicidality, and substance use.

Readings (Yoga)

Greene, D. (2021). Yoga: A holistic approach to addiction treatment and recovery. OBM Integrative and Complimentary Medicine, *6* (4), 1–8.

This brief article provides a condense summary of how yoga may be helpful in relation to addiction treatment and 12-step recovery.

Wasson, R. S., Dietrich, K. -M, Munjal, V., & Potts, A. A. (2024). Counseling patients on yoga with cultural humility to improve health equity: A guide for clinicians. *Journal of Health Service Psychology*, *50* (4), 188–197.

This article summarizes yoga practices, provides literature on yoga's impact on mental health, and cultural factors to consider.

WORKBOOKS/EXERCISES

Connors, G. J., Donovan, D. M., DiClemente, C. C., & Velasquez, M. M. (2015). Substance abuse treatment and the stages of change (2nd ed.). Guilford.

This book's section on group treatment presents "resolution-enhancing" exercises that can assist clients in addressing their ambivalence about their alcohol and drug use (good or less good things about use, decisional balance, looking back/looking forward, exploring goals, the "miracle question").

Corey, G., Corey, M. S., Callanan, P., & Russell, J. M., (2014). Group techniques (4th ed.). Brooks/Cole.

This book focuses on techniques used by the authors in groups. It encourages the use of techniques as a means to establishing therapeutic and human rapport between leaders and members.

Velasquez, M. M., Cronch, C., Stephens, N. S., & DiClemente, C. C. (2015). Group treatment for substance abuse: A stages of change therapy manual (2nd ed.). Guilford.

This book has three sections: The first section provides an overview of the stages of change model, and the next two sections (thinking about changing; making the changes) cover the stages of change, providing thorough outlines for each session.

ICEBREAKER EXERCISES

Group Therapy Focus

Group Therapy Card Deck: CBT, DBT, ACT and Positive Psychology Tips and Tools. Available at amazon.com

This icebreaker includes different types of counseling focus.

Individual Therapy Focus (can be adapted to groups)

We're Not Really Strangers. Available on amazon and werenotreallystrangers.com

In this icebreaker, there are questions on each card.

The Set Boundaries Deck. Available on amazon

Here there is an inclusion of scenarios and questions about boundary setting.

Talking Point-Small Talk. Available at talkingpointcards.com

These cards contain 200 small talk questions.

WEBSITES

General

American Counseling Association (ACA)
Association for Specialists in Group Work
www.asgw.org

This website is the home page of this division of the ACA that one can join by joining the ACA and thereby receive a division journal publication. It is committed to empowering counselors with knowledge, skills, and resources to conduct group work that is effective, socially just, and ethical. The division encourages diversity and multicultural involvement and has a drop-down menu of resources.

American Psychological Association (APA)
Division 49, Society of Group Psychology and Group Psychotherapy
www.apadivisions.org/division-49/index.aspx

This website is the home page of this division of the APA that one can join by joining the APA. This division assists in the development and advancement of group psychology and group psychotherapy. Its purpose is to promote group development and the group psychology field through research, teaching, education, and clinical practice. The website has numerous resources such as publications (e.g., journal, newsletter).

National Association of Social Workers (NASW)
www.socialworkers.org

Although this organization does not have a specific chapter for group work, by accessing the drop-down menu under "Practice," the behavioral health section contains topics on substance use and other addictions, and the clinical social work section has information on group therapy.

Music Therapy

www.musictherapy.org

This website for the American Music Therapy Association, Inc. (AMTA) has a 3-page article on music therapy and addiction treatment (2021 pp. 1–3) that can be accessed through https://www.musictherapy.org/assets/1/7/FactSheet_Music_Therapy_and_Addiction_Treatment_2021.pdf

Transgender

https://www.apa.org/topics/lgbtq/transgender-people-gender-identity-gender-expression

The APA website includes an article that answers commonly asked questions related to the transgender population including the difference between sex and gender, "types of transgender people," and the discrimination faced by the transgender population. They also include a list of external resources regarding transgender health, advocacy, and human rights.

https://www.counseling.org/docs/default-source/competencies/algbtic-competencies.pdf

The ACA includes competencies and best practices when working with the transgender population. This includes using the competencies and various different counseling settings as well as during individual, family, and group work.

https://glaad.org/transgender/transfaq/

The GLAAD website has a helpful transgender FAQ that addresses pronoun uses, how to treat transgender individuals with respect and information on being an ally to the transgender community. They include resources for transgender individuals as well as allies to the trans population.

https://www.mayoclinic.org/healthy-lifestyle/adult-health/in-depth/transgender-facts/art-20266812

The Mayo clinic provides a brief overview of helpful terms related to transgender and gender diverse populations. They discuss issues such as sexual orientation and gender dysphoria to provide an introduction of language and terms.

https://www.socialworkers.org/Practice/LGBTQIA/Sexual-Orientation-and-Gender-Diversity

The NASW website has a Practice Section of LGBTQIA2S+ on Sexual Orientation and Gender Diversity. In this section they discuss the ethical responsibility of advocacy (with a link to tools and resources to support this population); inclusive language; results of the 2022 National Survey on LGBTQ Youth Mental Health; and NASW Advocacy Highlights.

https://southernequality.org

The southern equality website is a multipage website that includes LGBTQIA+ friendly events happening in the south United States. They also have a list of description of all the projects they are working on the support and advocate for LGBTQIA+ individuals. This website includes a donation option to support their funding and resources on how to become involved in the community or allies.

https://transequality.org/issues/resources/understanding-transgender-people-the-basics

This website is a resource for A4TE (Advocates for transequality). The website includes resources on the political, health care, and various other issues that impact the transgender population. This website is information heavy with resources for financial support as well as basic "Trans 101" education.

https://ustranssurvey.org

The website for the 2022 U.S. Trans survey shows early findings for the largest survey "of trans people, by trans people" in the United States. The website includes quotes.

CLASSIC FAVORITES

READINGS

Kelin, R. H., & Schermer, V. L. (Eds.) (2000). Group psychotherapy for psychological trauma. Guilford.

This book focuses specifically on trauma in terms of group work.

Malekoff, A. (2004). Group work with adolescents: Principles and practice 2nd ed. Guilford.

This book has 17 chapters on group work with the adolescent population. Chapter 9 has an appendix that provides information on group manuals specifically designed for this age group.

Rogers, C. (1970). Carl Rogers on encounter groups. Perennial.

This book provides an overview of encounter groups.

Substance Abuse and Mental Health Services Administration. (2005). *Substance abuse treatment: Group therapy: Treatment improvement protocol (TIP 41) series* (DHHS Publication No. SMA 05-3991). Rockville, MD: Author.

This book has seven chapters that discuss substance abuse treatment groups in general, types of common groups, placement criteria for clients, group development and tasks, stages of treatment, group leadership, and training/supervision.

White, J. R., & Freeman, A. S. (2000). Cognitive-behavioral group therapy for specific problems and populations. American Psychological Association.

This book provides a cognitive–behavioral focus on group work.

WORKBOOKS/EXERCISES

Carrell, S. (2010). Group exercises for adolescents (3rd ed.). Sage.

This book provides numerous exercises for working with adolescents.

DeLucia-Waack, J. L., Bridbord, K. H., Kleiner, J. S., & Nitza, A. G. (2006). Group work experts share their favorite activities: A guide to choosing, planning, conduction, and processing (rev. ed.). Alexandria, VA: Association for Specialists in Group Work.

This 189-page workbook has group activities for each stage of group development (i.e., orientation, transition, working, termination).

Dossic, J., & Shea, E. (1988). Creative therapy: 52 exercises for groups I. Sarasota, FL: Professional Resource Exchange.

Dossic, J., & Shea, E. (1990). Creative therapy: 52 exercises for groups II. Sarasota, FL: Professional Resource Exchange.

Dossic, J., & Shea, E. (1995). Creative therapy: 52 exercises for groups III. Sarasota, FL: Professional Resource Exchange.

Each of these books has 52 exercises that are clearly described in terms of how to use them in a group context.

Fleming, M. (1995). Group activities for adults at risk for chemical dependence. Minneapolis, MN: Johnson Institute.

This 113-page workbook has numerous exercises that can be used in a group setting for substance-abusing clients.

Greanias, T., & Siegel, S. (2000). Dual diagnosis. In J. R. White & A. S. Freeman (Eds.), Cognitive-behavioral group therapy for specific problems and populations (pp. 149–173). Washington, DC: American Psychological Association.

This book chapter provides group assignments for a dual diagnosis group.

Ingersoll, K. S., Wagner, C. C., & Gharib, S. (2002). Motivational groups for community substance abuse programs. Richmond, VA: Mid-Atlantic ATTC (804-828-9910). mid-attc@mindspring.com https://people.uncw.edu/ ogler/mi%20groups%20for%20com%20sa%20prog.pdf

This book addresses the application of Motivational Interviewing in group therapy with substance abusers.

Metcalf, L. (1998). Solution focused group therapy. Free Press.

This book addresses the application of solution-focused therapy in a group setting. It has an excellent admission interview form and forms for notes for the client and therapist to complete after each session to monitor clinical work from a solution-focused perspective.

Mueser, K. T., Noordsy, D. L., Drake, R. E., & Fox, L. (2003). Integrated treatment for dual disorders. New York, NY: Guilford.

This book has a helpful section (four chapters) on group interventions with persuasion, active treatment, social skills training, and self-help groups when working with dual-disordered clients.

Ragsdale, S., & Saylor, A. (2007). Great group games. Minneapolis, MN: Search Institute.

There are 175 exercises formed around the stages of group development that can be used for all ages.

Rohnke, K., & Butler, S. (1995). Quicksilver. Dubuque, IA: Kendall/Hunt.

This book consists of activities and adventure games that can be used with groups.

ICEBREAKER EXERCISES

Chat Pack. Available at www.questmarc.com

These cards each have a question on them.

Conversations to Go. Available at www.moonjar.com

These cards come in a box (encouraging people to think outside of the box), and each has a question written on it.

Soul Cards 1 & 2. Available at www.touchdrawing.com

These picture cards can be used to facilitate discussion.

The Feelings Playing Cards. Available at www.timepromotions.com

Each card has a cartoon face and an emotion written on it.

Printed and bound by CPI Group (UK) Ltd, Croydon, CR0 4YY

25/07/2025

14708841-0001